Lucid Food

Lucid Food

COOKING FOR AN ECO-CONSCIOUS LIFE

Louisa Shafia

photographs by JENNIFER MARTINÉ

TEN SPEED PRESS
Berkeley

Published in the United States by Ten Speed Press, an imprint of the Crown Publishing Group,

a division of Random House, Inc., New York.

www.crownpublishing.com

www.tenspeed.com

Ten Speed Press and the Ten Speed Press colophon are registered trademarks of Random House, Inc.

Library of Congress Cataloging-in-Publication Data

Shafia, Louisa.

  Lucid food : cooking for an eco-conscious life / Louisa Shafia ; photography by Jennifer Martiné.

      p. cm.

  Includes index.

  Summary: "A collection of healthy, seasonal, eco-conscious recipes, plus sustainable cooking, lifestyle,

and entertaining tips"—Provided by publisher.

  1. Cookery (Natural foods) 2. Sustainable living. I. Title.

  TX741.S493 2010

  641.5'636—dc22

                         2009012404

ISBN 978-1-58008-964-7

Printed in China, text printed on recycled paper (60% PCW with soy-based inks)

Cover and text design by Toni Tajima

Photography assistance by Stacy Ventura

Food styling by Karen Shinto

Food styling assistance by Jeffrey Larsen and Fanny Pan

10 9 8 7 6 5 4 3 2 1

First Edition

Contents

Spring · 105

Summer · 141

Accompaniments | 177

Resources | 193

Acknowledgments

I would like to thank my mother, Georgia Shafia, for teaching me how to cook and entertain with style and originality. Thank you to all the Shafias, Schafiyhas, and Shafiihas, especially Ammeh Melih, for your unconditional love and for exposing me to Persian food and culture.

My heartfelt thanks to Brie Mazurek; I'm happy my proposal fell into the hands of an editor who cares deeply about the issues covered here. I'm grateful to Sara Golski, Aaron Wehner, Debra Matsumoto, Patricia Kelly, Kristin Casemore, and everyone at Ten Speed Press for their enthusiastic support. Special thanks to art director Toni Tajima for incorporating a variety of viewpoints and ideas into one beautiful vision.

Thanks are due to my three muses, whose superior senses of taste and style I've been lucky to have at my disposal: Jennifer Revit, for her golden palate and honest opinions; Julie Byun, for her willingness to advise even from across the country; and Olga Naiman, for going above and beyond in her generosity as a friend and collaborator. My thanks to Eric Tucker of Millennium Restaurant for setting an indelible example of what a good chef should be. I am also grateful to Michael Psaltis, my agent, for guiding me through the writing process with patience and humor. My army of recipe testers provided invaluable insights: thank you all for your spirit of adventure. A big round of applause goes to the hardworking chefs and servers who helped to pull off all of the wonderful Lucid Food events. I raise a glass of sambuca to Rachael Ray and John Cusimano for their generosity and support.

Finally, my gratitude goes to James Rotondi for in-house editing, endless comic distractions, and for whisking me away on vacation when I didn't know how badly I needed it.

Introduction

On a sunny summer afternoon in 2003 I was taking the subway from Brooklyn to Manhattan when suddenly the lights and air-conditioning went out and the train, thankfully still in the station, came to an abrupt halt. After an announcement that a power outage had taken place, the doors opened and everyone exited the train and went back out to the street. Little did we know that this was the beginning of a now-legendary two-day multistate blackout, which tangled public transportation, made life difficult for many elderly people, and inconvenienced millions.

Ironically, it was anything but a dark evening for many New Yorkers. Instead, as twilight fell, there was tangible excitement in the air, with countless people getting an unexpected night off and pouring out onto the streets to share a sense of wonder and adventure. Because my phone was out, I walked to my nearest friend's house and called up to his window. He ran down and together we excitedly explored the impromptu street party that was taking place on the sidewalks.

Neighbors were chatting with neighbors; restaurants had set up grills out front and were selling cold beer from tubs of ice; bars and stores were lit with candles; and later there was a marching band parading through the crowds, and even fireworks! It was one of the best nights I've ever spent in New York, a special evening when the modern world of bright lights, cable TV, and fast food took a backseat to genuine face-to-face interaction, simple pleasures, and the rediscovery of a true community spirit. And, for the first time in years, a near-full moon was the only big, bright light shining in New York City.

Practical magic

With this book, I'd like to convey the essence of what I learned that evening. Something truly magical emerges when we slow down, turn off our modern gadgets, and approach the shared rituals of food—procuring, preparing, cooking, and even cleaning up—with an appreciation for its timeless role in our daily lives and its relevance to our community and our planet. *Lucid Food* is about enjoying the sensuousness of food, while cooking and shopping with an eye toward conservation and social conscience. This book includes more than eighty-five healthful, seasonal recipes that will guide you toward making earth-friendly choices about what you prepare for meals—and, just as importantly, *how* you prepare them.

As we watch our economy—one based largely on cheap energy—reach its breaking point and we begin to reexamine the foundation of the so-called "American way of life," our habits will have to change. Although many of the luxuries we've come to take for granted in the past fifty years have been wonderful, there has also been a downside—namely, the ease with which we're now able to isolate ourselves in our individual homes, and to insulate ourselves from friends and neighbors, through the use of air-conditioning, television, and the Internet. While such modern conveniences certainly provide us with many benefits, one could argue that an overreliance on technological advances may actually be making our lives less fulfilling, not more.

There are those who will counter that the act of "going green"—cutting back sharply on cheap fossil fuels and taking serious steps to conserve in our daily lives—will require a joyless rejection of the twenty-first-century good life, but that's not supported by what many of us experienced when the lights went off in New York City. Quite the opposite: By practicing conservation, returning to a "waste not, want not" mindset, and savoring both our food and our free time, we enrich our lives through a greater sense of connection and responsibility to other people.

Besides, we may have no choice. Making these kinds of lifestyle changes seems increasingly imperative in order to protect our planet and revitalize our economy. What's more, we've been made painfully aware of the tragic health consequences of the American diet here and in other countries that have adopted our eating habits. Large portions of meat, fried foods, and a lack of fresh produce have led to obesity, diabetes, cancer, heart disease, and stroke. We are being challenged to change our lifestyles and our diets because of mounting problems that have resulted from our overconsumption and waste, and the prospect of "going green"—once seemingly trendy—is now more of a necessity than a curiosity.

Still, whether by reducing our use of electricity, driving less, entertaining in a "waste-free" fashion, or buying locally grown foods, we'll find plenty of advantages and rediscover many long-forgotten joys through making some simple, life-affirming changes.

Growing up green

I grew up in a house where we nearly always ate healthy, fresh food and were "eco-friendly" long before it occurred to anyone to use that term. It wasn't that we were especially ahead of our time; rather, my parents didn't quite realize that the Depression had ended, so absolutely nothing went to waste. My father grew up in Iran during World War II. He told me stories of eating government rations like bread that came with little surprises like shoelaces and buttons—baked right in!

When he first came to this country, my father couldn't believe the abundance of every kind of food—not to mention the ready availability of meat—and so, during my parents' first years of marriage, he ate a dinner of steak and white rice every single night, just because he could. At some point, however, his family history of high cholesterol and heart disease started to catch up with him, and our family reverted to eating much

the same way he had when he was growing up (minus the shoelaces, thankfully). Our standard dinner was rice cooked with lentils, fresh herbs, and onions (the inspiration for the Green Rice recipe on page 190), a big salad with oil-and-vinegar dressing, and seared chicken or fish. For dessert—oh, how I hated it—we ate fresh fruit.

My mom grew up in Philadelphia with a victory garden that my grandfather still lovingly tended when I was little. She was always proud of growing her own beautiful tomatoes in our backyard, along with lettuce and carrots. She looked forward all year to the raspberries that fruited on an ancient vine against the fence. Even though we were by no means poor, cards and gifts were always homemade, and we wore hand-me-downs or bought clothing from the dreaded House of Bargains. Thriftiness was alive in the kitchen, too. My dad chronically overate because my mom would beg him to finish up leftovers so she wouldn't have to throw food away.

Like most American kids, I found plenty of ways to gastronomically rebel against these old-fashioned ideas. But thanks to my upbringing, fresh vegetables are still my comfort food, and I make a point to reuse plastic bags, carry my own thermos, and seek out vintage clothes. Those Depression-era habits were genuinely eco-friendly, and nowadays, that hard-won knowledge is being dusted off for a new generation. With my own catering company, Lucid Food, as well as through my work at forward-thinking restaurants like San Francisco's Millennium and New York eateries Aquavit and Pure Food and Wine, I've experienced firsthand how a cuisine based on the simple virtues of fresh, local foods and ethical consumption can please the most discerning palates while contributing to a better future for our planet.

Bringing it all back home

Now is an excellent time to proudly reclaim old conservation-minded food traditions, many of which are disdained by a consumer culture that revolves around instant gratification. This book is a celebration of those time-honored traditions, including gardening, composting, foraging, reusing glass bottles, salvaging, preserving food, and eating local foods, all of which used to be a part of daily life and are now being rediscovered. Fortunately, an unexpected by-product of taking up the mindful habits of our grandparents is that, despite their occasional austerity, these simple practices can enrich our lives, improve our communities, and enhance our connection to the cycles of nature.

Old-fashioned habits are clearly coming back into style. To take only a few examples, there's the Edible Estates project started by artist Fritz Haeg, which encourages homeowners to grow food in their front yards instead of using pesticides to achieve the perfect green lawn. The Obama Administration took a cue from the country's best-known food activists, including chef Alice Waters and food and science writer Michael Pollan, and have turned part of the South Lawn of the White House into an organic produce garden. In several states, dairy farms are selling milk in reusable glass bottles with a refundable deposit. Around the country, whole municipalities and even big retailers are encouraging shoppers to suspend their use of disposable plastic bags and return to the custom of bringing their own cloth bags for shopping. From swap meets where used clothing is creatively recycled to houses built entirely from recycled materials, the conservation consciousness that seemed so basic to previous generations is finding a new voice in our own.

What is lucid food?

The mission of this book is to help you make great food in ways that will sustain you and the environment. *Lucid Food* is a collection of seasonal recipes interspersed with relevant and practical information on cooking and sourcing food with an eco-friendly approach. Among the topics explored to help you "green your cuisine" are: composting, growing your own food, finding animal products produced using sustainable methods, and low-waste shopping and entertaining. The book also provides you with real-world definitions of frequently misunderstood food terms like *organic* and *free-range*, and helps explain how the marketing uses of these words don't always square with their real-life meanings.

Lucid Food is organized into chapters by season, in order to show off the best ingredients that each part of the year has to offer. In a typical supermarket, we see the same goods all year long, regardless of the season. However, shoppers are increasingly aware that the strawberries and tomatoes they see on supermarket shelves in winter require a huge expenditure of resources to be ripened, stored, and flown to us from far-flung destinations. Many of these foods come from countries where labor conditions and pesticide use are unregulated. This produce is usually inferior to locally-grown fruits and vegetables in both taste and nutritional value.

Every season offers us unique edible treats, such as persimmons in fall, red kuri squash in winter, morel mushrooms in spring, and berries in summer, and *Lucid Food* allows each season its turn at center stage. Supermarkets only sell summer foods in the dead of winter because *we buy them*. But as we begin to understand that there are uniquely delicious, easy-to-prepare seasonal foods available to us all year-round, we can change our shopping habits and, ultimately, alter the very fabric of food commerce.

Now, you will see a few tropical items in the following recipes, including bananas, chocolate, vanilla, cashews, tamarind, and galangal. We are a diverse country with a worldly palate, and humans have a natural yen for tastes and textures that aren't native to their own land. After all, the ancient network of trade routes known as the Silk Road facilitated the exchange of goods between the East and West for thousands of years.

Fortunately, when it comes to exotic foods, a little goes a long way, so our appetite for imported delicacies doesn't need to have a strong negative impact on the environment. But we should make an effort to think of these long-distance foods as special treats, and we shouldn't be surprised if we have to pay a high price for them. It's my belief that by understanding the real costs in energy expenditure and environmental degradation linked to eating exotic foods, we will treasure them even more.

The recipes throughout *Lucid Food* are made from whole, unprocessed ingredients. For the most part, the dishes are quite healthful—human health, after all, corresponds directly to the health of the planet. The more we foster biodiversity and support the preservation of small farms, woodlands, clean waterways, and an environment free from pollution, the healthier we'll be as a population, both in body and in mind.

Several of the recipes do call for animal products. I considered including only vegetarian recipes, as first-hand experience has taught me that a vegetable-based diet can be enormously satisfying and healthful. Still, I wanted to include recipes with animal products because many of my favorite vendors at the farmers' market are suppliers of eggs, chicken, fish, cheese, and meat. Preparing a home-cooked meal with the most flavorful meat or the freshest fish is an important way to stay emotionally connected to our food, and these farmers are helping shoppers make the connection between buying locally and eating the best food possible. Moreover, it is vital to support small, ethical suppliers of animal products so that there remains a viable alternative to factory farms.

Paying to eat your ideals

Some will argue that eating local, sustainable, and organic food is simply too expensive—or, worse, exclusive or elitist—and that families on fixed incomes can't afford to eat this way. I would like to challenge that misconception right off the bat. First, the health and environmental costs of the traditional American diet are almost too numerous to mention. Cheap and processed foods carry a catastrophic price tag in epidemic health problems like obesity, attention deficit disorder, decreased immunity, heart disease, and diabetes, conditions for which each of us pays handsomely in taxes and skyrocketing health-care premiums. Inferior foods flown in from distant countries also carry massive hidden costs in the form of the petroleum and electricity required to transport and store them.

The fact is that there are many ways to "green" your diet affordably, and the benefits are myriad. Surely, every child deserves to eat fresh, nutritious food, and instilling healthy dietary habits in young children is a gift that will pay dividends throughout their lives. But the benefits of eating locally grown foods go beyond individual health; quite literally, the health of the nation is at stake. In recent years, we've seen how national food security is better served by local food sources; in the event of a national emergency, for instance, if our food supply is centralized somewhere far away, how will people eat? Food poisoning epidemics regularly make headlines, but they'd be far more preventable if food sources were more localized. Small, local producers have a shorter distribution and production trail, which makes tracing potentially tainted food much easier.

When it comes to costs, remember that buying local keeps money within the local economy. When shoppers buy food from a small farmer at the farmers' market, they are directly supporting that farmer, along with the person hired to work the farm stand and the network of local businesses that benefit from farmers' market shoppers—not to mention supporting the preservation of farmland and open space. Items at the farmers' market may be more expensive than the same items at the supermarket, but for anyone who wants to eat well and eat responsibly, there are options: One way is to join a CSA (Community Supported Agriculture) program, where shareholders invest in a farm and the return is a weekly box of high-quality produce at wholesale prices. Or why not grow your own food, either on the windowsill, in your backyard (if you're lucky enough to have one), or in a plot in a community garden space? What about keeping a few chickens so you have a fresh supply of eggs? Urban gardeners all over the country have garnered attention for beautifying neighborhoods and bringing low-cost fresh food into their communities. For the truly adventurous, there is always the option of foraging, still done regularly by all sorts of people, from Chinatown dwellers who collect ginkgo nuts to explorers in metropolitan parks picking apples to hikers who gather berries and mushrooms.

Aside from the actions that we as individuals can take, our elected representatives could clearly be doing a lot more to subsidize sustainable agriculture so that healthy foods are affordable for everyone. Currently, the U.S. government offers its assistance almost exclusively to the industrial agriculture giants who grow commodities using conventional—and damaging—pesticide control and energy-intensive production methods. Our tax dollars fund these subsidies that allow mega-producers to keep their prices low while small farms struggle on their own with little to no government support. That's where you come in. As more and more people make the switch to healthier, safer, locally grown foods, small farmers and the people who buy their food will have a bigger say in how farm subsidies are doled out. The momentum will build for a fundamental change in the way our leaders approach this crucial issue. Just as importantly, the more consumer demand builds for locally grown products, the more suppliers will bring these goods to the marketplace, helping bring prices down for everyone.

My hope is that the ideas in this book will make it easy for you to try new ingredients and cooking techniques while practicing conservation in the kitchen and at the market. I want to share the tips for healthy cooking and living that I've learned at home and in the world of professional cooking, and give you the confidence to interpret these ideas in your own unique way. Be adventurous, have fun, and enjoy finding the balance that works for you.

Eco-Kitchen Basics

In this chapter, I'll share all of my tried-and-true methods for putting a beautiful meal on the table while keeping a clear conscience. If you're willing to make some small changes, it's easier than you might think. Obviously, you can't always get to the farmers' market, and sometimes you'll forget your canvas shopping bag. But if you start integrating these habits into your routine, you'll find that you significantly reduce the amount of waste usually generated by shopping for, preparing, and serving a meal. A glossary of food terms is included to help you navigate any food market with authority.

Waste not, want not

There are lots of different ways to practice sustainability, and in fact every meal can be an act of environmental preservation, from the ways you acquire, eat, and clean up after your meals, to the example you set for the people around you. When I see wastefulness, I feel it viscerally, and I will go to great lengths to avoid creating waste myself.

It's not always easy. Often an impulsive purchase at the farmers' market causes me to abuse a perfectly lovely purse by insisting on filling it with raw produce and other messy foods rather than allowing one more plastic bag to find its way into my home. I'll go many thirsty hours without hydration if the only available beverage container is yet another disposable plastic bottle. Did I mention the hours I spend waiting in line at the well-meaning but chaotic food co-op so that I can buy olive oil and other staples in bulk in order to avoid excess packaging? Sure, my personal standards may be outside the norm, but I suspect they're becoming increasingly common. In fact, the more all of us speak up about our "waste-not" goals, the more accepted these ideas will become, helping broaden the spectrum of environmentally responsible choices available to consumers.

Here are some easy tips for shopping, cooking, and eating in a way that has as little impact on the environment as possible. Choose the ones that make sense for you, and keep the environment in mind, but don't torture yourself if you can't always be 100 percent green: People will be more likely to follow your example if you seem happy and calm . . . and your purse is in beautiful condition.

Five habits for eco-friendly food shopping

Keep the following practices in mind when planning menus, shopping for food, and dining out. If you have a good farmers' market or a conscientious food co-op that sells meat and seafood as well as produce, then most of the work is done for you. If you have to search farther afield for what you need, however, these simple guidelines will help keep you on the straight and narrow in your goal to buy eco-friendly foods.

1. SHOP LOCAL

Buying from local farmers helps to support the preservation of small farms and undeveloped land. And not only does local food taste better and have higher nutritional value because of its freshness, but you know exactly what you're getting—unlike with products from far away, where details about pesticides, land use, and working conditions are hard to come by. In contrast, local farms are transparent places where people are usually welcome to buy goods or take tours. Look for locally made goods at the supermarket, too: Some stores are making an effort to highlight local providers, even giving them their own section. Let shopkeepers know what you want by spending your dollars on local goods.

2. BUY ORGANIC FOODS

It's common to see organic foods at the supermarket, but don't rely on the label alone. The organic food label is quite controversial these days, as I discuss in the definition of "organic" in this chapter. Organic food is grown without pesticides, but it can have other environmental drawbacks. Food labeled "organic" often comes from large farming operations that devastate the earth where it's grown; is flown in from thousands of miles away, creating more carbon emissions; and is processed to stay preserved during

transport. The organic label can help you navigate your way around a conventional grocery store, but it's worth investigating the organic brands that you like and checking out their environmental record.

3. SERVE SEASONAL PRODUCE

Try to eliminate out-of-season produce, such as asparagus and strawberries in winter, that must be brought in from far away. Reducing air and ground transport for food cuts our use of fossil fuels and alleviates air pollution. And if you're looking to save money, seasonal foods are the cheapest choice: join one of the underground fruit exchanges that are popping up around the country like veggietrader.com or neighborhoodfruit .com where you can find local produce for free or at nearly no cost; or walk through the farmer's market at closing time to find deals from farmers who would rather unload ripe items than take them back.

4. CHOOSE ECO-FRIENDLY FISH

Consult the online seafood guides (page 194) when planning a menu. Do some research to discover which species are being fished or farmed using conscientious practices. Make a list and bring it with you to the market, so you know what to look for at the seafood counter or in the frozen seafood section. And remember, you can always buy canned or jarred sardines or anchovies—safe choices every time.

5. EAT LESS MEAT AND BUY RESPONSIBLY

Animals raised for slaughter in a free-range manner put less wear and tear on the ground where they're raised and require fewer or no antibiotics. Animal waste that's free of antibiotics and chemicals is friendlier to groundwater, plants, rivers, and wildlife. Because of the methane from their manure and the energy needed to grow and transport their feed, the world's livestock accounts for 18 percent of greenhouse gases, more than all forms of transportation combined (*New York Times*, October 9, 2008). Two to five times more grain is required to produce the same amount of calories from meat as from eating the grain itself. Buying meat from small farmers with sustainable business practices and reducing your meat intake can significantly help the environment. For more on animal products and their effects on the natural world, see the Winter chapter.

A dozen ways to reduce waste

As you begin your new green shopping regimen, you may find that practicing some of the tips below will earn you weird looks from store employees and shoppers. Don't worry: New ideas are often looked at with mild suspicion, and even simple changes like the ones outlined here can seem like extra work to overworked staff. Fortunately, people adapt. The idea of bringing your own bag for grocery shopping once seemed radical, but it's become an everyday habit for millions of people. So when shopping with the environment in mind, be brave, organized, and patient with people who may have a different point of view, all of which will go a long way toward convincing people of the worthiness of your cause.

1. BRING YOUR OWN BAGS AND CONTAINERS

Plastic bags, cardboard containers, and plastic boxes have a long life span. Reuse old plastic bags for holding vegetables and bulk goods when shopping. And then use them again; all they need is a quick rinse or dusting-off between uses. At the farmers' market, transfer berries out of their cardboard or plastic boxes into a lightweight sealable container and give the disposable box back to the farmer. When buying eggs, bring the carton back to the farmer. At the Union Square farmers' market in New York, some farmers give a reimbursment for returned egg cartons and cardboard berry boxes. Ideally, it's good to take along several reusable, washable cotton produce bags. These can be found at health food stores and online.

2. BRING A CONTAINER FOR LEFTOVERS TO RESTAURANTS

If every time you go out for Chinese food you're unable to finish what you ordered, bring along a sealable container and put leftovers in it at the end of the meal. This is a simple way to avoid taking home that cute Chinese food carton, plastic soy sauce packet, bag, fork, and knife, all of which will go into a landfill. Not so long ago, people didn't leave bread in the bread basket at a restaurant but instead took it home, as the idea of throwing away good food was unheard of. (Interestingly, in Europe, restaurant servings are not as large as they are in the United States, so take-home containers are practically nonexistent. And in many countries, like Italy, bread costs extra.) I have even brought my own container to the gelato shop on the corner to avoid using the standard disposable plastic cup with a plastic spoon. (Yes, I did get very strange looks, but I was able to have my ice cream and eat it, too!)

3. CARRY A STEEL THERMOS

How often do you buy a cup of coffee to go? Or a plastic bottle of water at the beginning of the day, or when setting out on a hike? Cups and bottles get discarded, and even the few that get recycled still carry a high cost in the fossil fuel production required to make and transport them, as well as in the recycling process itself. By contrast, a steel thermos is light and easy to sanitize—just wash it out after using, and boil the parts every few weeks. Such a small act could make a huge difference to the environment. As more people are putting this method into practice, more coffee shops around the country are encouraging the trend by giving a discount for bringing your own thermos.

4. CARRY YOUR OWN SILVERWARE

Even at the most eco-conscious health food restaurants and buffets—where they admirably serve food on compostable paper plates—plastic cutlery and disposable chopsticks are often used. All of that plastic, paper, bamboo, and wood ends up in a landfill. Carrying a personal set of cutlery as an environmental act started several years ago in China, where activists have taken to bringing their own reusable chopsticks stored in cloth bags into restaurants, in the hope of preserving some of the 25 million trees that are cut down each year to make chopsticks. It's easy to fashion a makeshift carrying case by wrapping cutlery in a clean dish towel, or get fancy and make a washable cloth pouch that snaps shut. This small act could make a big change; activists in South Korea have succeeded in getting disposable chopsticks banned in many restaurants, where metal ones are now used instead.

5. AVOID USING PLASTIC AROUND FOOD

Plastic food storage containers can leach many harmful toxins into food. Aside from harming our health through contact with our food, plastic has many other unfortunate characteristics: It releases chemicals such as benzene and dioxin into the air as it is manufactured; it is largely considered disposable; it takes hundreds of years to decompose; and it remains a danger to the water table once it's in a landfill. Happily, there are several viable alternatives to plastic food storage containers, such as glass, metal, and ceramic bowls with plastic lids. These choices are all heavier and more expensive than plastic, but they are safe and will last indefinitely.

6. BRING YOUR LUNCH TO WORK

Instead of buying lunch on the go, spend twenty minutes the night before packing a homemade lunch. This is a great way to avoid all the extra packaging that accompanies takeaway, and at the same time save enough money for a meal in a nice restaurant once a week. There are many alternatives to carrying your lunch in plastic containers. Pyrex bowls with plastic lids are a good choice, and stainless-steel "tiffin" sets with several stackable bowls, like the ones used in India, can be found on the Internet. Food-safe ceramic containers are another option. For wrapping sandwiches, the washable Wrap-N-Mat, available through online retailers, closes with Velcro and unfolds so it can be used as a placemat.

7. SOAK BEANS AND GRAINS BEFORE COOKING

Soaking certain foods reduces cooking time as well as gas or electric use. In the case of beans, which soak up a lot of water as they cook, it can also mean less water use. It takes only a few seconds to throw a cup of beans or grains into a bowl of water before going to bed, and it will cut the cooking time by half. But even soaking for an hour can make a big difference. This method applies to noodles, lentils, and white rice, foods that you wouldn't normally think to soak. If you have trouble getting beans to cook all the way through, try boiling them for 10 minutes, then letting them soak in the hot water with a tablespoon of apple cider vinegar for 1 to 12 hours. Drain and then cook the beans as usual. Another energy-saving approach is to use a pressure cooker. Pressure cookers cook foods in roughly a third of the time required for conventional pots and pans. There are several high-quality models available that are either plugged in or used on the stovetop.

8. REDUCE OR ELIMINATE PAPER TOWEL USE

Like any paper product, paper towels are made from trees, and most wind up in landfills. Paper towels seem irreplaceable for certain tasks, but you can significantly reduce their use in the kitchen. A decent sponge can last a long time—simply boil it for a few minutes to kill germs and odors. Use a wire rack instead of paper towels for draining fried foods. For cleaning, check out microfiber cloths, which can be used multiple times; they are available in hardware and home supply shops as well as natural grocers. If you have to use paper towels, use ones made from recycled paper. Paper towels can be composted too, so unless you have a large amount, there's no need to throw them in the trash.

9. USE ALL OF YOUR FOOD

The average American household throws an estimated 14 percent of its purchased food into the garbage. This figure includes items that have never been opened, small amounts left in the bottoms of containers, and food that has simply gone bad. Clearly, there's money and resources to be saved here. Keep useful scraps like chicken bones, shrimp shells, or vegetable trimmings, all of which can be made into flavorful stocks; you can even use apple cores, tomato trimmings, corn husks, mushroom stems, and cheese rinds: simply cover the ingredients with water, bring to a boil, and simmer for approximately 15 minutes. (Some scraps, however, like kale stalks, will become bitter, so do a little research if you're new at making stock.) Try to shop practically, and only buy produce when you know you'll have time to cook; fresh food can go bad quickly. Find out which parts of your produce are edible, and enjoy unsung tasty ingredients— such as beet greens, broccoli stalks, or squash seeds—that often get thrown away. And what you can't use, compost.

10. SHOP IN BULK

Bulk shopping helps to eliminate excess packaging and saves money. Both traditional supermarket chains and boutique health food stores sell food in bulk, but it's not an option in enough stores. If the store where you shop sells food in bulk, bring paper or plastic bags for items like bread, grains, and other dry goods. Standard half-pint-, pint-, and quart-size bulk containers can be reused for buying olives and other non-dry bulk items. If you don't own standard-size containers, bring glass jars or other portable containers. Make sure to weigh them and label them clearly with their weight measurements.

11. RECYCLE CANS

A trip to the supermarket means I come home with some recyclable containers, usually aluminum cans. It's especially important to always recycle cans because it's an extremely energy-efficient process: According to the Environmental Protection Agency website, recycling an aluminum can will save 95 percent of the energy needed to make the same can from its virgin source. That's a pretty good ratio.

12. BIKE, WALK, OR TAKE PUBLIC TRANSPORTATION

Finish off your shopping trip with a walk, bike ride, or train ride home so as not to consume too much fossil fuel transporting groceries. While shoppers on foot certainly can't stock up on groceries the same way that drivers can, they can benefit by making more frequent, smaller shopping trips, placing an emphasis on fresh, local, and seasonal foods. In most of the world, it's customary to shop for food several times a week, but many Americans prefer to shop in fewer, bigger installments. It could be argued, though, that paying more attention to the foods you buy and devoting a bit more time to shopping and cooking can help you to slow down and appreciate the food on your table—as well as enjoy better health and a richer quality of life.

Why organic isn't always the best choice

My catering clients often request that their food be "all organic." To them, this means a guarantee that they will be eating the best food possible, and doing so with a clean conscience. I always explain that I will use as many organic ingredients as I can, but that my priority is buying local. Here's why.

Most of the food I cook with comes from farmers who can't afford to meet national organic standards, yet their food is often tastier and more pure than food that's labeled "organic." This can be confusing, because not long ago, the term "organic" implied that a food came from a small farm where few, if any, pesticides were used, and farming was conducted with the goal of being good to the land as well as profitable. Since then the volume of food labeled "organic" has increased dramatically, yet food packaging depicting bucolic settings would have us believe that it still comes from those same small farms. The truth is that in order to supply enough goods to superstores like Wal-Mart, organic has gone corporate, and most food labeled as such is grown as a monocrop on vast industrial farms and transported long distances, while soil erosion results from the intense demands made on the land to grow crops in large volume year round.

There are approximately two million farms in this country—that's down from the roughly five million we had in the 1930s. At that rate of closure, I want to do what I can to help small farms stay afloat, even if they are not certified organic. Their products are more interesting than mass-produced organic goods as well. Even if purple fingerling potatoes or garlic ramps aren't on everyone's shopping list, they have a following at the farmers' market, and that's enough to sustain the business of the small producers who grow them. If we were limited to buying only certified organic foods, we would no longer have access to all of the eclectic, colorful choices that make American cuisine what it is today.

Must-buy organics

In an ideal world, every item in every market would be organic in the best and broadest sense of the term. Truly organic food—free of pesticides, hormones, additives, and genetically modified organisms and produced without harmful environmental practices, unsafe working conditions, or mistreatment of animals—would be the only choice, and it wouldn't be outrageously priced. It's a lofty goal, but as people speak up, a more transparent and healthy food supply is taking shape. For now, though, it's too inconvenient and costly for most of us to buy only organic, and we often have to sacrifice our ideals. In my own life, there are certain foods that I would rather not eat if I can't find them with an "organic" or other specialized food label. The following foods are the ones I won't compromise on.

FAIR-TRADE ORGANIC BANANAS

One of our favorite fruits, the banana, has a bruised and spotty history of environmental pollution and unethical labor practices. Most that we see on U.S. store shelves come from plantations in Central America where workers may make as little as $2 a day and are exposed to toxic pesticides and fertilizers. Not only do these chemicals harm workers, but they also endanger surrounding wildlife, particularly the North American songbirds that winter there. In contrast, bananas labeled "fair trade" are produced with the restricted use of agrochemicals and the workers are paid fair wages; growers deal directly with U.S. importers, cutting out the middlemen who take a large percentage of the sale. If you can't find fair-trade bananas, try to buy organic rather than conventional. Sure, organic bananas are more expensive, but if you eat one or two fewer per week, the cost ultimately evens out.

Sadly, we may not have bananas around much longer. A half century ago, the Gros Michel variety was the Western world's most popular banana, reputedly sweeter and richer than the Cavendish kind that we eat today. Like the Cavendish, the Gros Michel was grown as a monocrop. Lacking genetic diversity, it was vulnerable to blight and was wiped out by the fungus called Panama disease (for more on the importance of plant biodiversity, see the section on heirlooms, page 108). In recent years, a new strain of the fungus has decimated banana production in Asia, and it may only be a matter of time before the rest of the world's plantations are attacked. Botanists are working to develop new breeds in case the Cavendish disappears, but it may be time to develop a taste for plantains and other banana varieties. For dessert and drink recipes that call for bananas, try substituting an equivalent amount of papaya, avocado, cooked winter squash, or cooked plantain, adjusting the sweetness as needed.

PASTURE-RAISED, SMALL-FARM POULTRY AND EGGS

If you live near a factory poultry or egg farm, be on your guard. Conditions near these windowless bunkers are so awful that in the past decade several lawsuits have been brought against their operators by citizens and environmental groups. Neighbors complain of insect infestations, noxious odors, and epidemics of fish deaths caused by water pollution from waste runoff. In Maryland, the Chesapeake Bay is now so polluted with runoff from chicken farms that the crab population has fallen by 70 percent, and oysters are down to 1 percent of historic levels. In recent years, substantial press attention has focused on the humane issues of such operations, where egg-laying chickens have their beaks removed with a heated blade and spend their lives in cramped cages.

Chickens and eggs are sources of cheap, low-fat protein, but the low prices are made possible only by the abuse of the birds and the environment. In contrast, pasture-raised birds that roam freely on small farms, eating their natural diet of grass and insects, spread their manure evenly over the soil, making it a natural fertilizer instead of a waste problem. Chickens and eggs from small farms cost more to produce and may seem expensive, but we get what we pay for in better-tasting products, a healthier environment, and good neighbors.

The truth is, we don't need to eat a lot of eggs and chicken. Instead of buying breasts, try cooking a whole chicken and using the parts for soup, stir-fries, and sandwiches. You'll get several meals out of the chicken, and the cost per meal will be much cheaper. You might buy pricier eggs from pasture-raised chickens, but eat fewer of them. Breakfast is our most egg-intensive meal, but there are loads of other delicious possibilities for a satisfying start to the day, as you will see throughout the book.

ORGANIC OLIVE OIL

Because I consume it in such volume, drizzling it on soups and salads in addition to using it for cooking, I want my olive oil to be free from chemicals. Commercial olive oil production uses many pesticides that spread through the air well beyond the treated areas. These chemicals pose a health threat, as the residue on treated olives can enter the oil and even increase in concentration when the olives are pressed. In light of Europe's olive oil scandal of 2008 (Italian producers reportedly mixed soybean and other oils, dyed them green, and sold them as extra-virgin olive oil), it's wise to go with an organic producer that can verify details about where and how its oil is made.

Organic olive oil is expensive, but there are ways to get around the high price. Many co-ops sell bulk organic olive oil, and major grocery chains sell it at a discount under their own label. You can also buy directly from a wholesale distributor of organic products—something you'll want to do with friends or office mates, as you'll need to meet a price minimum in order to buy. When buying oil in bulk, store the extra in glass jars in the refrigerator to prevent it from going rancid. When you need more, simply let it come to room temperature and pour out enough to last for a few weeks.

FAIR TRADE ORGANIC COFFEE

Conventional coffee is usually grown in open fields requiring intensive treatment with chemicals. Organic coffee, however, is grown under trees, so that the beans receive shade and nitrogen, and leaf litter fertilizes the soil naturally. Because of the intensely harmful impact on birds of the chemicals used to grow conventional coffee, organic fair trade–certified coffee is recommended by the Audubon Society, the American Bird Conservancy, and the Smithsonian Migratory Bird Center. Luckily, fair trade organic coffee is ubiquitous these days at many cafes and retailers, and not only does it taste good, but you can enjoy your daily brew even more knowing that fair trade growers in farmer-run cooperatives are guaranteed a fair market price for their coffee. The benefits of fair trade coffee are threefold: a better life for the families in Africa and Latin America who grow the coffee; fewer pesticides released into the environment and near workers; and superior-tasting coffee.

LOCAL, IN-SEASON, ORGANIC BERRIES

We've gotten used to seeing berries in the store all year-round. In spite of the weak flavor of out-of-season berries, they still sell well. Fruit grown out of season is flown to us from tropical climes, requiring a huge expenditure of fossil fuels. But in addition, berries are one of the most heavily sprayed of any crop. The United States Department of Agriculture has rules about what pesticides can be used for agriculture in this country, even though many Americans consider the rules not nearly strict enough. In Latin America, however, where many of the berries on our shelves are grown, growers may legally use pesticides that are forbidden here, including chemicals rated Class 1 toxins by the World Health Organization.

It's impossible to wash off all pesticides, especially from a fruit like a strawberry, which can't be peeled. I settle for buying nonorganic berries at the farmers' market during the summer. I trust that the farmers I speak to every week aren't putting high concentrations of toxins into the food I'm buying, and if they are, at least I am only indulging myself for a few months a year. As an alternative, try growing your own organic berries. In winter, avoid lackluster berries and choose seasonal fruits like pomegranates, citrus, and persimmons instead of berries; you may find you like them just as much.

UNPROCESSED, ORGANIC SUGAR

Because of the environmental fallout from sugar production (see "Earth-Friendly Alternatives to White Sugar," on page 68), as well as its quick-hitting effect on blood sugar, I avoid buying conventional white sugar. If I need a dry sweetener for baking, there are several options, including date sugar and maple crystals, but plain organic sugar is still more eco-friendly than the nonorganic white variety. Organic sugar is grown without synthetic fertilizers or pesticides, using methods that prevent soil erosion.

When craving store-bought sweets like ice cream or cookies, choose items that list organic sugar in their ingredients. Many brands have begun using organic sugar in their products, spurring industry heavyweight Domino to produce a version made from sun-sweetened sugarcane grown without pesticides. This groundbreaking change in the industry came about through consumer demand—remember, your voice has an impact.

If cost concerns and availability are forcing you to decide which foods to buy organic, keep these choices in mind. Even if these are the only organic foods you insist on, you will be making a significant positive impact on both your own health and the health of the planet. And keep the slightly increased cost in context; as the saying goes, "You get what you pay for." The only reason non-organic foods have traditionally been so cheap is that the environment itself has been shortchanged. With organic, fair trade, and pasture-raised foods, we are finally paying the real—and perfectly reasonable—cost of producing earth-friendly foods, and treating nature as a valued partner.

Eco-foodie words to watch

The eco-friendly food movement has a language all its own, and it's good to be familiar with some of the most commonly used terms. Here is a glossary of food labels, shopping buzzwords, and food-related environmental terms that will give you a handle on the vital discussions about food and conservation that are taking place in the media, at restaurants, on farms, and in home kitchens.

BIODIVERSITY

A contraction of "biological diversity," this term refers to the wide range of plants and animal life that nature supports, and the genetic variety and richness that environmentalists are working to protect. The more biodiversity we have, the healthier the planet will be. For example, healthy populations of pollinators like bees, birds, and bats help to ensure flourishing trees and plants in our fields and forests. Living organisms, ecosystems, and biological processes all depend on each other for survival. Human activities like pollution and development are largely responsible for diversity loss on land and in water. There is a growing awareness that we must do more to protect the amazing variety of animals and wild places still left by enacting environmental legislation, planting heirloom fruits and vegetables, supporting farmers who grow heirloom produce and animals, and—perhaps most importantly—eliminating pesticide use.

BIODYNAMIC

The label "biodynamic," which you will see on food as well as wine labels, refers to a method of agriculture that is much more stringent than what the USDA requires for organic certification. It is a highly developed approach to growing that calls for raising animals and plants on the same farm, using the stars to determine the planting and harvesting calendar, and applying only natural preparations for weed control and fertilization. Many of the practices used in biodynamic farming sound like witchcraft to modern ears, such as making a compost preparation from oak bark that has been placed inside the skull of a domesticated animal and buried underground. But studies have shown that certified biodynamic farms tend to have highly fertile soil, and their environmental track record is usually outstanding.

CAGE FREE

This is a marketing term applied to eggs from chickens that have been raised in open barns instead of battery cages and that have continuous access to the outdoors. This is not a term defined by the USDA, so it is not regulated, and farms that claim to be cage free are not inspected. "Access to the outdoors" can mean that there is one small door for thousands of hens, or that the outdoor area is a concrete lot. According to the Humane Society, a cage free environment is a step up from cages, but it basically means that thousands of chickens are crammed into an open space rather than in individual cages, so it doesn't ensure sanitary conditions or a cruelty-free environment.

CARBON FOOTPRINT

The website www.carbonfootprint.com defines the term as "a measure of the impact our activities have on the environment, and in particular climate change. It relates to the amount of greenhouse gases produced in our day-to-day lives through burning fossil fuels for electricity, heating and transportation, etc." For example, if someone eats a lot of meat, drives a gas-guzzling car, chooses old-growth wood products for home furnishings, and leaves the air-conditioning on when not at home, that person will have a larger carbon footprint. The "footprint" is a convenient image for measuring an individual's environmental impact, and for figuring out ways to make it smaller.

COMMUNITY SUPPORTED AGRICULTURE (CSA)

In a Community Supported Agriculture plan, known as a CSA, members pay a fee to join a farm, and in return receive a weekly box of food. CSA members invest in the farm with their membership money, so the farmer has start-up funds to begin the season. The "share boxes" are the return on the investment. When joining a CSA, it's possible to buy into just one farm, or a group of farms, so members can conceivably get produce, eggs, dairy, and meat all from one CSA. There are more than two thousand CSAs in the United States, mostly serving urban centers. For help finding a CSA in your area, see the Resources section on page 194.

CONCENTRATED ANIMAL FEEDING OPERATIONS (CAFO)

This is the official Environmental Protection Agency (EPA) term for large factory farms where animals are stocked in high density. Since their inception, CAFOs have been widely criticized for their treatment of animals. Recently, however, the CAFO system has been identified as one of the worst environmental offenders, and as a major culprit responsible for endangering the food supply. The huge amounts of corn and soy grown to feed animals in CAFOs—a drastic altering of their natural diet—account for a large percentage of the petroleum-based fertilizers and pesticides used in this country.

Antibiotics are routinely used in livestock feed, bringing about the evolution of drug-resistant bacteria as well as outbreaks of salmonella and E coli poisoning. The high concentration of animals in factory farms leads to accumulations of manure that can't be absorbed by the land; the waste piles up, giving off ammonia and other gases. It leaches into the water table and washes into rivers and streams, creating aquatic dead zones. Because of their poor energy efficiency, high pollution output, abuse of animals, and inability to ensure food safety, CAFOs are generally regarded as outmoded.

CONVENTIONAL FARMING

Though it sounds old-fashioned, this term actually refers to today's standard agricultural methods, including chemical and synthetic pesticides and fertilizers, large tracts of land devoted to a single crop, and CAFOs, where animals are crowded into close quarters. The term is defined in contrast to more eco-friendly farming methods, such as organic, biodynamic, or pasture raised.

FAIR TRADE

The fair trade system was created to help disadvantaged farmers in developing countries who grow products such as bananas, coffee, tea, sugar, vanilla, rice, wine, and chocolate for export to developed countries. The FT symbol signifies that the product meets the following criteria: the farmers receive a fair price for the product; workers labor under safe conditions, meaning no exposure to toxic pesticides; no child labor is used; producers sell directly to importers, avoiding middlemen; and environmentally sustainable farming methods are used. Certified FT producers are inspected and must meet rigorous guidelines in order to participate in the system.

FREE RANGE

Usually used in reference to poultry, this label means that the animal was able to walk around freely. But as with "cage free," there is no standard definition of the term, and its use is unregulated, so this label may not mean a great deal.

GENETICALLY MODIFIED

When referring to a product like cotton, corn, or rice, this term means that the genetic structure of the plant has been altered by insertion of a gene from another plant or even an animal. The goal of gene altering is to give a plant characteristics that it doesn't naturally have, such as the ability to resist pests, endure drought, or, in the case of the Flavr Savr tomato—the first genetically modified (GM) food to be granted a license for human consumption—the ability to last longer on a store shelf than a normal tomato. The practice is highly controversial because the long-term effects of growing and eating GM foods have not been tested. A well-known study in 1999 showed that pollen from GM corn killed monarch butterflies. When GM crops are planted, their seeds blow into nearby farms and enter non-GM crops, so it's hard for nearby farmers to make sure the crops they grow are "clean." Incredibly, producers aren't required to label genetically modified foods in the United States, so consumers don't know which products have been modified. Unlike the United States, the European Union, Japan, and Australia all require labels on GM foods.

GRASS FED

This food label refers to meat from animals that roam on pasturelands. Grass is the natural diet of ruminant animals, although in the modern feedlot they are fed primarily on genetically modified grain and soy, along with other cheap fillers including garbage and chicken waste. Grass-fed meat costs more but contains more vitamins and less fat, and is better for animals and the environment. Pasture-raised animals release less methane into the air and fertilize the ground evenly with manure, and their grazing has been shown to increase the amount and hardiness of native plants. Grass feeding serves a dual purpose: improving land quality and restoring wildlife habitat, while producing high-quality meat.

HEIRLOOM

Heirlooms are garden plants passed down through generations, selected for their taste, beauty, and ability to thrive. Some people define heirlooms as seeds older than fifty years. Heirlooms naturally develop resistance to the pests and diseases with which they evolve, and each variety is genetically unique. These plants are extremely important because they help to preserve genetic diversity, protecting food crops that would otherwise be wiped out by disease and infestation. Heirloom animals are also referred to as "heritage breeds" and are valued for the same reasons as heirloom plants. Read more about planting heirlooms on page 108.

LOCAVORE

This term, coined in 2005, refers to someone who only eats food that has been grown or raised within a 100-mile radius. Locavores argue that buying from nearby food sources helps to reduce carbon emissions by cutting down on transportation, and routes consumer dollars toward small farms, resulting in preserved farmland and an economic boost to local communities. Cultivating these more direct relationships with local producers, locavores insist, improves food safety and producer accountability, and well-informed consumers help to foster the kind of public awareness that keeps food production in line with environmental goals.

ORGANIC

The definition of organic agriculture is controversial. Originally, *organic* simply meant producing good food through sustainable methods, such as planting crops on a rotating basis to enrich soil, using chemical-free pest control and fertilization, and raising livestock in open pasture without hormones or antibiotics. In essence, organic farming was practiced by small farmers who thought of themselves as stewards of the land. The term's current meaning, as defined by the USDA, has many loopholes that may unfairly benefit corporations. These days, food may legally be labeled organic even if its growing procedures deplete soil, synthetic ingredients are added to the finished product, and the animals (in the case of meat or dairy) never go outside. The substantial fee and detailed record keeping required by the USDA for a food producer to receive organic certification have forced many small and truly sustainable farmers out of the business. Ironically, organic agriculture began as a grassroots movement set in opposition to the mechanized and chemical-laden production methods pushed by the very same corporations that now dominate the so-called organic market.

Large corporations are typically driven by profit, not by an interest in the environment. While there may be exceptions, as a rule, the "organic" label simply means that certain minimal standards were met in order to slap on the "organic" label and charge consumers a higher price. For the conscientious shopper, the safe bet is to buy directly from small farmers whom you can talk to and even visit on their farms if you wish. That's the best way to verify a food's authenticity.

PASTURE RAISED

This term conveys the same idea as "grass fed," but refers to poultry, too. This label means that animals roam freely outside and eat a natural, species-appropriate diet.

SUSTAINABLE

In a general sense, this term refers to any system that operates in a way that doesn't deplete the earth. When applied to food, it means producing and eating food in balance with environmental limits, recognizing the needs of nonhuman species, and planning with the long term in mind, so that the natural world may be preserved intact for generations to come. An example of eating sustainably is consuming meat in small amounts and choosing meat from farms where animals are raised on pasture.

USDA CERTIFIED

The United States Department of Agriculture (USDA) is the government office in charge of establishing policies on farming, agriculture, and food. Like any government agency, this department is bogged down with bureaucratic systems, is influenced by industry lobbyists, and is partial to the politics of the current presidential administration. The USDA has been widely faulted for overlooking egregious offenses in CAFOs, allowing GM crops to be planted without adequate testing or supervision, and watering down the definition of organic to favor big business over environmental protection.

WILD FORAGED

Wild-foraged foods are edible plants found in nature, including berries, mushrooms, herbs, fruits, and nuts. There is renewed interest in these foods, as people are making an increased effort to eat locally and choose food sources with minimal environmental impact. Restaurant chefs have championed this revival, highlighting on their menus wild-foraged foods like morel mushrooms, garlic ramps, and fiddlehead ferns.

fall

As the weather gets colder, a warm room filled with people, food, and drink takes on a novel allure, and social events fill the calendar with increasing frequency until they reach their holiday peak. All of this makes fall a perfect time to try out innovative ways of entertaining and sharing meals. In this chapter, you'll find ideas for organizing inexpensive, eco-friendly gatherings with an emphasis on bringing people together around simple, seasonal food. During harvest season, the beautiful produce of summer bursts forth one last time with a fierce blast of flavor before going dormant for the winter. Traditionally, people living in temperate climates have used fall days to preserve fresh fruits and vegetables. (See page 177 for easy recipes for savoring the harvest flavors after the temperature drops.)

In the fall, nature demonstrates how composting works; leaves fall to the ground to form a nourishing layer as we enter the period of decay that allows the earth to replenish itself and bloom anew in the spring. Happily, we can follow this example all year round. In this chapter, you'll learn how the simple act of saving vegetable scraps can help to abate our landfill crisis, and you'll find practical tips for setting up your own compost.

No-Waste Entertaining

My New York City catering company, Lucid Food, first gained attention for our no-waste approach to catering and entertaining. We were asked to cater a picnic for the United States Green Buildings Council, the architects' association that sets "green" building and construction standards. They wanted to hold a gathering that conformed to their mission statement of sustainability, and they were dedicated to making the idea work.

Together we produced an event that surprised and delighted the guests, and not a single item went into a landfill afterward. The lovingly handcrafted food included mulberries shaken from trees in Hudson River Park, scapes (young garlic shoots) picked on a friend's farm in Chappaqua, and hawthorn berries from northern Pennsylvania. The event was a great success and earned considerable attention from the press. Following are the guidelines we used to make the event completely waste-free.

All of the suggestions from the Eco-Kitchen Basics section (beginning on page 9) can be applied here, too. If you use even a few of these suggestions, not only will you avoid creating garbage that ends up in a landfill, but you'll save on the amount of energy and fossil fuels used to produce the event. Most of these approaches are suited to home entertaining, but many can be applied to full-scale catered events as well.

MENU

- **Buy organic** when it's local and in season. See page 9 for more about eco-friendly food shopping.
- **Serve mini fruits.** There are many local fruits that are only big enough for a few bites, like Seckel pears, lady apples, kumquats, and small plums. These can be served whole for a fruit dessert. Cut fruit turns brown after a short time and leftovers are usually thrown away, but beautiful intact fruits can be served later or taken home by guests.
- **Serve homemade drinks** like lemonade and iced tea instead of buying them in containers that will later be disposed of or recycled.

AMBIENCE

- **Serve food using real plates, glasses, napkins, and utensils, not disposables.** If you're throwing a big event and it's in your budget, rent these items from a party rental company, which can drop off the clean equipment and then pick it up the next day. Some companies will let you pick up and drop off equipment yourself in exchange for a reduced price. You don't even have to wash anything; just put everything back in their crates. If it's impossible to use real plates, use biodegradable materials instead of plastic or Styrofoam. There are some really lovely choices available now, including plates made from bamboo or palm leaves. They can be composted after the meal.

- **Use locally grown,** chemical-free flowers from the farmers' market. Compost them afterward or send them home with guests.
- **Use recycled glass bottles** for serving beverages and as flower vases.
- **Use flower petals and fruits** to decorate the table. One of my favorite combinations for a winter table is pomegranates, small red apples, and dried rose petals. During the holidays, shiny silver bowls piled high with red pears, apples, and cranberries look festive and elegant. In summer, fresh flower petals, bright red cranberry beans in their pods, and the pink and green stalks of rhubarb are my favorite choices. Fresh chile peppers are also a beautiful choice, coming in red, purple, green, and orange—a great choice as long as your guests don't take a bite!
- **Use soy wax and beeswax candles or LED lights** to illuminate the space. Soy wax candles are biodegradable, while beeswax candles are free from chemicals and use natural fiber wicks, and LED lights consume less power than regular lightbulbs, lasting approximately 20 times as long.

CLEAN-UP

- **Recycle** all glass bottles after use.
- **Share.** If you make a lot of food, ask guests to bring food containers so they can take home leftovers. You put a lot of love into this food, so don't let any of it go to waste.
- **Return** any containers from the farmers' market to the farmers.

I keep a one-gallon clear plastic compost container on the kitchen counter when I cook, and instead of throwing scraps into the trash, I throw them into my compost bucket. When it's full, I empty it out at the farmers' market compost drop-off. Between composting and recycling, I almost never have to take out my garbage. But there are lots of other ways to compost, too. For instance, if you have a yard, try mixing your vegetable scraps with dirt and leaves and let it sit, turning it every so often, until it turns into a rich black soil. For the brave, or especially teachers with classrooms, there is worm composting, where you put red wriggler worms, vegetable scraps, and soil into a ventilated box for composting indoors. If you're interested, there's a wealth of information on composting. For indoor worm composting, the best place to start is with Mary Appelhof's kid-friendly instruction book *Worms Eat My Garbage: How to Set Up & Maintain a Worm Composting System*. For outdoor composting, check with your local botanical garden or gardening community for regionally specific guidance, or go online for more information.

With its citywide composting program for private residences and businesses alike, the city of San Francisco has set a precedent for closing the recycling loop. The compost is made into nutrient-rich, water-retaining soil that is used by area farms and vineyards to produce the food and wine sold at restaurants and food stores back in the city. This is an ideal solution for keeping all the food discarded by private homes and food businesses from taking up room in landfills. As author Michael Pollan points out in his essay, "Farmer in Chief," if we could adapt this closed-loop model on a national scale, we would shrink our garbage output, reduce the amount of water used for irrigation and our use of chemical fertilizers, and increase the nutritional content of our food supply all in one fell swoop (*New York Times*, October 9, 2008).

Elderberry Cold Tincture

In fall, look for clusters of deep purple berries on elderberry trees growing wild throughout the country. I've seen elderberries for a fleeting harvest week at farmers' markets, but you can buy dried organic elderberries as a substitute. This powerful tonic has worked effectively for me over the last two winters; I take a tablespoon right when I feel a cold coming on, and I keep taking it every few hours until I feel better. It's very tasty, too! **Makes 5 cups**

2 cups fresh or dried elderberries	1 cup honey
2 cups vodka	

Rinse the elderberries in cold water and remove any large stems. Place the elderberries in a glass jar. Add the vodka and honey and shake well. Seal the jar tightly and store, unrefrigerated, in a cool place for 6 weeks, shaking the jar once or twice a week.

Set a strainer in a bowl and line it with several layers of cheesecloth or a coffee filter. Pour the contents of the jar through the strainer, pressing the berries with the back of a ladle to extract all of the potent juice. Pour the strained tincture into a clean glass jar and store in the refrigerator, where it will keep indefinitely.

Buckwheat Crepes with Mashed Potatoes and Jack Cheese

Buckwheat adds a delicious sour note to crepes and breads. As a crop, buckwheat gives a boost to the environment because it suppresses weed growth and provides nectar for honeybees. It requires little to no chemical fertilization and actually adds nutrients to the depleted soil on which it's grown. I like to fold these savory whole-grain breakfast crepes in half, but they can also be filled and rolled like sushi. For a spicier version of this dish, add red pepper flakes. Makes 8 crepes

3/4 cup plus 1 tablespoon buckwheat flour

1/3 cup white flour

1/2 teaspoon salt

3 large eggs

2 tablespoons olive oil, plus more for brushing

4 cups Watercress Mashed Potatoes (page 185), or regular mashed potatoes

1 cup shredded Monterey Jack cheese

2 cups Cilantro-Jalapeño Sauce (page 184)

To make the batter, mix the flours and salt in a large bowl. In a separate bowl, whisk together the eggs, olive oil, and 1 1/2 cups water. Add the egg mixture to the flour mixture and whisk until the batter just comes together. Cover the batter and let it rest in the refrigerator for 2 hours.

Preheat the oven to 425°F.

Heat a lightly oiled skillet over medium heat. When the pan is hot, drop 1/4 cup of the batter into the skillet, immediately tilting and rotating the pan to spread the batter evenly. Cook the crepe for roughly 1 minute, until it is set on the bottom, then gently loosen the edges with a heatproof spatula and flip. Cook on the second side for 30 seconds, or until firm. Slide the crepe onto a plate and repeat with the remaining batter.

Line a baking sheet with parchment paper. Place a crepe flat on a cutting board and place 1/3 cup of the mashed potatoes on one half of the crepe. Scatter 2 tablespoons of the cheese over the potatoes, followed by a pinch of salt, and fold the crepe over the filling. Place the filled crepe on the baking sheet. Repeat with the remaining crepes.

Lightly brush the crepes with a little olive oil and bake for 8 to 10 minutes, or until the tops are golden and the cheese is melted. Serve hot with the sauce poured on top.

Amaranth:
A Vital Grain, Rediscovered

Amaranth, a nutty-tasting alternative to oatmeal, has more protein, fiber, and amino acids than most other grains. The tiny grains are sold in most natural food stores. The mild green and red leaves of the plant can also be prepared like spinach—look for them in Latin and Indian food stores. As more farmers return to old-fashioned crop rotation to improve soil quality and break insect and disease cycles, alternative crops like amaranth are being swapped in for wheat. Amaranth's deep taproot has been shown to improve soil quality and boost production of whatever crop is planted subsequently. Amaranth's growing role in agriculture means more of a presence on store shelves and in American cooking.

Although it may seem exotic, Amaranth is native to nearby Central America, probably Mexico, where it was once cultivated widely. Amaranth played a crucial role in the ceremonies of Aztec religion; statues of the Aztec gods were made from amaranth mixed with blood or honey and eaten, often as part of the ritual of human sacrifice. In his mission to destroy Aztec civilization and convert Mexicans to Christianity, the Spanish conqueror Hernán Cortés banned the Aztecs from growing the grain on pain of death, so the amaranth fields were burned and amaranth's existence obscured in what would later become American territory. Amaranth grains and leaves, however, are still used widely in Mexico, Peru, and Ecuador, and the leaves are popular in China, Africa, and India, where the plant was transported.

33

Amaranth Porridge with Fruit and Nuts

Try making a soothing bowl of cooked amaranth for breakfast. Enhance it with classic oat-meal toppings, from milk and fresh fruit to a pat of butter and a pinch of salt. Soak the ama-ranth in water overnight to cut the cooking time in half. **Serves 4 to 6**

1 cup amaranth grains	Chopped nuts
TOPPINGS	Vanilla extract
Milk	Ground cinnamon
Maple syrup	Ground nutmeg
Seasonal fruit	

Soak the amaranth grains overnight in 2 cups water.

Place the amaranth grains and their soaking water in a small saucepan (use 3 cups water if the grains weren't soaked overnight). Turn the heat on high and stir until it comes to a boil. Decrease the heat and simmer, stirring frequently, until the porridge thickens, about 12 minutes. (If the grains weren't soaked, the cooking time will be about 20 minutes.) Serve the porridge in a bowl with your choice of the toppings.

Tortilla Española

Tortilla Española is an indispensable dish: It makes a great breakfast, goes well in a sand-wich, and makes a hearty hors d'oeuvre when cut into small squares. The only challenge is removing the tortilla from the pan intact, but you can cheat by waiting until it's cold. Embel-lish the tortilla with Stinging Nettle Pesto (page 115), Cilantro-Jalapeño Sauce (page 184), or plain ketchup. For a light meal, serve the tortilla alongside the Puntarelles with Anchovy Dressing (page 156) and fresh bread. **Serves 6**

1¹/₂ pounds Yukon Gold potatoes	Salt and freshly ground black pepper
5 tablespoons olive oil	6 eggs, lightly beaten
4 scallions, green and white parts thinly sliced	¹/₄ pound Havarti or other mild cheese, finely diced

Preheat the oven to 400°F.

Peel and quarter the potatoes. Cut the quarters into slices ¹/₄ inch thick. Heat a large ovenproof sauté pan over high heat and add 3 tablespoons of the olive oil. Add the potato slices and cook until lightly browned, about 5 minutes. Decrease the heat to medium and cook, stirring frequently, until a fork sinks into the potato slices easily. Remove the potato from the pan and set aside.

Return the pan to medium heat and add the remaining 2 tablespoons olive oil. Add the scallions and sauté until tender and lightly caramelized. Decrease the heat and add the potatoes. Season with salt. Spread all the vegetables evenly across the pan and pour the eggs over the vegetables.

Sprinkle the cheese evenly over the eggs and bake for 15 minutes. The surface should be firm and springy. Loosen the edges from the pan with a knife and flip the tortilla onto a plate to serve, or flip it after it has cooled.

The tortilla may be served hot or at room temperature. Slice into wedges and sprinkle with pepper before serving.

Chickpea Cakes

Serve these fragrant Indian-spiced cakes with sweet and tangy Cilantro-Jalapeño Sauce (page 184) to set off their flavor, and Cucumber Yogurt (page 184) for a creamy contrast. For a hearty lunch, perch a few cakes on top of a green salad, or pack them into a pita pocket along with shredded vegetables. Makes approximately 10 cakes

2 tablespoons olive oil, plus extra for frying	2 tablespoons dried mint
1 yellow onion, minced	1 teaspoon ground turmeric
2 cloves garlic, minced	$1/8$ teaspoon cayenne pepper
2 jalapeño peppers, seeded and diced	2 cups cooked chickpeas
2 tablespoons ground coriander	2 teaspoons salt
2 tablespoons ground cumin	1 egg, lightly beaten
	1 cup bread crumbs

Heat a large skillet and add 2 tablespoons of olive oil, followed by the onion. Saute for 5 minutes, until soft, then add the garlic, jalapeño, coriander, cumin, mint, turmeric, and cayenne, and sauté for 2 more minutes. Remove from the heat, and stir in the chickpeas. Let cool.

Put the mixture in a food processor and pulse until the chickpeas are broken down, but the mixture still has texture. Fold in the salt, egg, and $1/2$ cup of the bread crumbs. Refrigerate the mixture for 20 minutes so it can firm up and cool completely, making it easier to form into patties.

Pour the remaining $1/2$ cup of bread crumbs onto a plate. Form 3 tablespoons of the mixture into a ball. Flatten the ball against your palm, shaping it into a cake. Dredge the cake in the bread crumbs. Heat a skillet with $1/4$ inch of olive oil. When the oil is hot, drop in several cakes and fry until golden brown, about 1 minute per side. Drain on a wire cooling rack. If you prefer to bake the cakes, preheat the oven to 425°F. Place the cakes on an oiled, parchment-lined baking sheet and brush each one with a little olive oil. Bake for 10 minutes, then rotate the pan and bake for 5 minutes, or until the cakes are brown on top and crisp. Serve hot.

Grilled Maitake Mushrooms

Start this recipe the night before serving so that the mushrooms can marinate overnight. Widely known as "hens of the woods" because of their richness and dense texture, maitakes can look intimidating, like a strange piece of brown coral. But they're delicious, meaty, and easy to work with. If you've never tried maitakes, I encourage you to experiment with them. Portobellos, shiitakes, or any mushroom big enough to grill may also be used. **Serves 4**

1 cup olive oil

$^1/_2$ cup soy sauce

2 scallions, green and white parts
separated and green parts thinly sliced

2 cloves garlic, peeled and crushed

2 tablespoons honey

5 tablespoons white wine

Salt and freshly ground black pepper

$1^1/_2$ pounds maitake mushrooms

$^1/_2$ bunch watercress, roots trimmed

Put the olive oil, soy sauce, scallion whites, garlic, honey, and 2 tablespoons of the wine in a blender and blend until smooth. Season with salt.

Cut the maitake into slices 1 inch thick. It's important that each slice be attached to the large stem at the bottom; otherwise the slice will fall apart and be hard to handle on the grill. To avoid this problem, simply pick up the mushroom and look at where the stem is. Turn the mushroom on its side while gently slicing, making sure the connection between the frilly part of the mushroom and the stem stays intact. Place the slices in a shallow rimmed dish and coat them with the marinade. Cover and refrigerate overnight.

Heat a grill until it's very hot and arrange the maitakes on the grill, reserving the marinade. Press the slices with a metal spatula to form grill marks, and brush them with some of the reserved marinade. Grill for 3 minutes, then turn and press down with the spatula again. Brush with some of the remaining marinade and grill for 2 minutes more. Set the maitakes aside.

Heat a sauté pan over high heat and add the reserved marinade and the remaining 3 tablespoons white wine. Bring to a boil and reduce for a few minutes, until the sauce coats the back of a spoon.

To serve, arrange a bed of watercress on four individual plates. Slice the maitakes into a few pieces and divide among the plates, arranging them on top of the watercress. Season with salt and pepper. Spoon the sauce over the mushrooms and garnish with the scallion greens.

Ginkgo Nut Dumplings
with Simple Dipping Sauce

Ginkgos are infamous for the acrid smell of their fruit, but the nuts hidden inside are a treasured ingredient in Asian cuisine. In and around the Chinatown neighborhoods of many cities, you can find people under trees collecting the nuts in autumn. Go out and join them, but be sure to wear protective gloves when touching the fruit and extracting the nuts; other-wise, the smell will remain on your hands. Remove the flesh outdoors—the less you bring into your home the better. You can find canned or dried ginkgos in Asian grocery stores. **Makes 24 dumplings**

1¼ cups ginkgo nuts	1 clove garlic, minced
3 tablespoons plus 1 teaspoon olive oil	1 bunch bok choy, green part only, coarsely chopped
Salt	1 tablespoon flour
3 scallions, green and white parts separated and thinly sliced	1 package round dumpling wrappers
2-inch piece fresh ginger, peeled and coarsely chopped	2 tablespoons apple cider vinegar
2 tablespoons mirin	2 tablespoons soy sauce
	Red pepper flakes (optional)

If you are using fresh ginkgo nuts, gently crack the shells. Blanch the nuts in salted water for 1 minute, then shock in ice water. Alternatively, toast the nuts in a dry skillet until they turn green. After blanching or toasting, rub off the papery skin using your fingers or a clean kitchen towel. If you are using canned ginkgos, simply rinse.

Heat a sauté pan over medium heat and add 2 tablespoons of the olive oil. Add the nuts and a dash of salt. Cook for 1 minute. Add the scallion whites, the ginger, and mirin and cook for 2 minutes. Add the garlic and cook for 1 minute more. Transfer the nuts to a plate to cool and return the pan to the stove. Add another tablespoon of olive oil to the pan and sauté the bok choy with a dash of salt until the leaves are cooked down to half their original size. The bok choy should be mostly dry when you add it to the pan; otherwise, the dumpling filling will be wet. Remove the bok choy from the heat and let cool.

Put the nuts and bok choy in the bowl of a food processor. Add all but 2 teaspoons of the scallion greens. Pulse until the mixture is blended but still chunky. Transfer to a bowl and season with salt.

In a small bowl, whisk the flour with 2 tablespoons water. Brush the edges of a dumpling wrapper with the flour paste. Place 1 tablespoon of the filling on the wrapper and fold the wrapper into a half moon. Press the edges to seal. Repeat with the rest of the wrappers and filling.

To make the dipping sauce, whisk together the vinegar, soy sauce, the remaining 1 teaspoon olive oil, and the reserved scallion greens. Add red pepper flakes if desired.

Steam the dumplings in a covered steamer basket for 4 minutes. Serve hot with the dipping sauce.

Roasted Beets with Persimmons over Market Greens

Luscious persimmon fruits blow in and out of markets in late fall. They grow wild in North America—I've found them while foraging in Maryland—but the native species is small and astringent. The two kinds found in stores are cultivars from Asia. Hachiyas are oval-shaped and must be completely soft, all the way down to the base, before being eaten. Fuyus, which look like flat tomatoes, are eaten firm. If you can wait until it ripens, the Hachiya has more flavor, but the Fuyu works just as well in this recipe. **Serves 4**

3 red beets, peeled and quartered

5 tablespoons olive oil

Salt and freshly ground black pepper

1 shallot, minced

2 tablespoons Dijon mustard

2 tablespoons apple cider vinegar

$1^1/_2$ tablespoons honey

2 ripe Hachiya persimmons

2 large handfuls lettuce greens, torn into pieces

$^1/_2$ cup toasted pistachios

Preheat the oven to 400°F.

Put the beets in a baking dish with 1 tablespoon of the olive oil, $^1/_4$ cup water, and a dash of salt. Cover the dish and bake for 40 minutes, until the beets are easily pierced with a fork. Let cool and slice the beets into wedges.

To make the dressing, put the shallot, mustard, and vinegar in a bowl and let sit for 15 minutes, until the shallot is softened. Whisk in the honey and the remaining 4 tablespoons olive oil. Add the beets to the dressing, and toss until they are fully coated; the dressing will turn a deep pink color. Taste and season with salt. The recipe can be prepared up to this point several hours in advance and stored in the refrigerator; the beets will soak up more flavor and the color of the dressing will intensify as they sit.

To serve, gently slice the persimmons into wedges. Divide the lettuce among four plates, and drizzle with a tablespoon of dressing from the bowl of beets. Place several beets on the lettuce, and arrange a few pieces of persimmon over them. Season with pepper. Spoon the dressing over the persimmons, and garnish with the pistachios.

Kale Salad with Avocado, Almonds, and Toasted Nori

Massaging kale (shown opposite) with olive oil and salt is a useful technique popular in raw cuisine. The greens get "cooked" by the salt and the squeezing action, becoming tender and more digestible. Nori seaweed, the kind used to wrap sushi, adds a rich, savory note to the salad. Find nori at natural food stores or Asian markets. In summer, add shaved radishes, fresh corn kernels, and mint leaves. **Serves 4**

1 bunch kale, thick stems removed and coarsely chopped	1 carrot, peeled and sliced into thin half moons
1 ripe avocado, diced	1 small sweet, crisp apple, sliced thin
Salt and freshly ground pepper	1 scallion, green part only, thinly sliced
1/2 clove garlic, minced	1 large handful toasted almonds
3 tablespoons olive oil	1/2 sheet nori

Place the kale in a large bowl with the avocado. Add a dash of salt, the garlic, and olive oil. Gently massage everything together for about 3 minutes. The kale will shrink and become darker and more pliable.

Reserve a small handful of the carrot and apple slices for garnish, then gently fold in the carrot and apple to the kale mixture. Taste and season with salt.

Divide the salad among four plates. Top each plate with the sliced carrots, apples, and scallions. Season with pepper. Scatter the almonds on top.

Turn a burner to medium heat, pick up the sheet of nori with a pair of tongs, and pass it over the flame 3 or 4 times. Let the nori cool for a moment, then fold the sheet in half lengthwise and cut with scissors along the crease. Using the scissors, cut several thin ribbons of nori over each plate. This salad can keep for up to a day in the refrigerator.

Seven-Vegetable Miso Soup

This brothy, colorful soup is a potent tonic that will cure what ails you. Miso paste, made from fermented soybeans, is an essential component of Japanese cuisine. As with yogurt and other fermented products, miso is most beneficial uncooked, so stir it into the soup only after turning off the heat. Wakame is a mild-tasting green sea vegetable most commonly used in the traditional miso soup that accompanies sushi. Burdock root (shown below) has a texture reminiscent of water chestnuts. It grows wild throughout the United States and can also be found in Japanese markets. After slicing burdock root, soak it in cold water to prevent it from turning brown. If burdock root isn't available, simply use more of the other vegetables.
Serves 4 as a starter, or 2 as a meal

1/2 cup burdock root, peeled and cut into 1-inch matchsticks

1 cup sweet potato, peeled and diced

1-inch piece fresh ginger, peeled and minced

2 scallions, green and white parts thinly sliced

1 teaspoon soy sauce

Salt

1/2 cup soft tofu, diced

6 shiitake mushrooms, stems removed and thinly sliced

1/4 cup sweet white miso

2 tablespoons dried wakame, soaked in 1/2 cup cold water

1 egg, lightly beaten (optional)

1 cup coarsely chopped fresh cilantro leaves

Put the burdock, sweet potato, ginger, scallions, and 5 cups water in a saucepan. Cover and bring to a boil over high heat. Decrease the heat and add the soy sauce and a dash of salt. Simmer, covered, for 15 minutes. Add the tofu and shiitakes and simmer, uncovered, for 5 minutes more.

Place the miso in a small bowl and add $^1/_2$ cup of the hot broth. Use a fork to break up the miso and whisk it until smooth. Drain the wakame and add it to the saucepan. Add the egg if using and stir. Turn off the heat and stir the dissolved miso into the saucepan. Taste and season with salt, if necessary.

To serve, divide the cilantro leaves evenly among the bowls and ladle the hot soup on top.

Red Lentil and Spinach Soup

Red lentils are quick-cooking beans, making them an obvious choice for last-minute meals. Their texture is starchier than regular lentils, and they have a light, sweet taste reminiscent of potatoes. For a creamier soup, add a dollop of Cucumber Yogurt (page 184). For a hint of spice, serve it with the Cilantro-Jalapeño Sauce (page 184). **Serves 4**

2 tablespoons olive oil	$^1/_2$ teaspoon ground turmeric
1 small yellow onion, minced	Pinch of cayenne pepper
2 tablespoons minced fresh ginger	1 cup red lentils
1 tablespoon ground coriander	2 cloves garlic, minced
1 tablespoon brown mustard seeds	Salt
1 teaspoon ground cumin	2 cups firmly packed spinach leaves, coarsely chopped

In a soup pot, heat the olive oil and add the onion. Cook, stirring occasionally, until the onion is translucent, about 5 minutes. Stir in the ginger, coriander, mustard seeds, cumin, turmeric, cayenne, lentils, garlic, and a dash of salt, and cook for 1 minute more.

Add 5 cups water and bring to a boil. Decrease the heat and simmer, stirring occasionally, until the lentils have cooked into a purée, about 20 minutes. Taste and add more salt, if necessary.

Just before serving, stir in the spinach and cook for 1 minute to wilt.

Potlucks, Picnics, and Supper Clubs

I love going out to restaurants to eat. Good food and wine, a welcoming staff, a pleasant ambience, and no cleaning up—what's not to like? Still, restaurants are no longer the only way, nor the most environmentally sound way, to dine out. Over the last few years, I've discovered that there's immense satisfaction in crafting your own special shared meal, or enjoying someone else's communal, creative supper.

A few years ago, some friends of mine in New York started a traveling potluck dinner called the Floating Feast. Each month, one of the thirty or so members of the group volunteers to host the event in his or her home. What ensues is a long, rollicking evening of heart-to-heart chats and unrushed group discussions. Guests migrate from chair to floor to standing with plates and drinks in hand against the backdrop of a homemade buffet comprised of dishes varying from the complex to the minimalist. Although the food is often quirky and the setting occasionally spartan, the cost is a fraction of that of eating out in a restaurant, and the experience is intimate and unimpeded by the standard restaurant time frame, which requires that servers "flip the tables" every 1½ hours or so.

One increasingly popular trend is the supper club or underground restaurant, where a meal is served in someone's home for paying guests. The person preparing the food may or may not be a trained chef, but he or she always knows how to cook.

For the last year, I've been visiting a supper club in a small house in Queens, New York. A few times a month, dinner is served to thirty guests for a reasonable $35; guests bring their own wine. At times, the food is stellar. At other times, it's less than perfect, but the host is a brilliant entertainer, and the strangers at the table are always interesting.

On special occasions, I drive out to an organic farm in New Jersey that has been holding these sorts of dinners for years. Once a month, the farmer invites a restaurant chef to cook a vegetarian meal for eighty people featuring produce grown right there on the farm. The meal is held in what was formerly a barn, lit warmly with white string lights. Guests sit at long communal tables and are served each course by a group of teenaged country kids and the farmer's own children. In the back, there is a broad table where you can refill your glass of homemade sangria. After dessert is served, there's a big bonfire outside that is perfect for tipsy philosophizing late into the night. (I will always be partial to this farm because on my birthday the farmer let me come and gather elderberries and black walnuts from trees on his property.) The experience of these farm dinners encompasses so much more than just food. They are an ideal way to get in touch with where your food comes from.

Beyond their social and culinary rewards, these alternatives to the conventional restaurant format touch on serious issues of sustainability, too. Fair labor practices, along with conditions that support the health of workers, families, and communities, are generally considered to be an essential part of long-term environmental solutions. It's common knowledge that most of the grueling physical labor necessary to operate a restaurant kitchen is often done by immigrant workers who are paid the minimum wage or less. Naturally, we should support restaurants that operate under good labor policies, and we should support legislation that seeks to change and improve poor working conditions. Just as importantly, supper clubs—unlike restaurants—encourage you to interact with the people who prepare your food and to mix with the people sitting all around you. More than just a night out, it's a way to build community and strengthen friendships, since sharing a home-cooked meal with someone tends to bring you closer.

ORGANIZING YOUR OWN EVENT

- **Start a potluck group with friends and rotate hosting duties monthly.** No one has to work too hard if everyone contributes a dish. To mix it up, pick a theme— food from the same country, food of a certain color, or food mentioned in a song—and choose a winner who fulfills the theme best. Have guests bring their own serving platters or bowls so all the cleanup doesn't fall to one person.

- **Have a picnic!** Scope out a friend's backyard or a local park. If there is a picnic table available, you can get fancy and use a tablecloth, place settings, candles, and flowers. You can make your favorite foods, enjoy uninterrupted conversation, and drink as many $10 bottles of wine as you care to. Bring food that is good eaten cold, unless you're also using a grill, in which case the possibilities are endless. A good way to make the event waste-free is for guests to bring their own real plates, silverware, and glasses. That way, no one has to haul around half of his or her kitchen.

- **Throw a nondenominational Shabbat dinner.** This is an idea I got from my friend Cat Greenleaf, who started these dinners in San Francisco and then brought them with her to New York. There is nothing specifically religious about the evening, but there is a strong spiritual element. Before the shared meal, everyone in the room says one thing that they are grateful for. It's a great way to start the weekend.

- If you have a generous host with a big kitchen, cook a meal together. Some people cook, some handle the decorations and setting the table, and some clean up. This is a great way to cook for a holiday dinner, when it's fun to spend the day whole day preparing everything at a leisurely pace.

Roasted Tomato and Goat Cheese Soup

In this recipe, pungent tomatoes are balanced by goat cheese for a rich fall soup. Goat cheese can seem pricey because, unlike cows, goats roam instead of graze in one spot. Due to their independent nature, goats can't be put into factory farms, which are cheap for farmers but hard on the environment. Most goat farms are small, family-run, and often highly sustainable operations. Find out about your local goat farm's practices and use their cheese in recipes like this, where a little goes a long way. Serves 4

12 ripe tomatoes	2 tablespoons balsamic vinegar
2 cloves garlic, peeled and smashed	4 tablespoons olive oil
1 yellow onion, coarsely chopped	Salt and freshly ground black pepper
1 tablespoon honey	1 dried bay leaf
2 sprigs fresh rosemary	$^1/_4$ cup fresh goat cheese

Preheat the oven to 425°F.

Core and quarter the tomatoes and scoop out the seeds, reserving the seeds and cores for the stock. In a large bowl, toss the tomatoes with the garlic, onion, honey, rosemary, 1 tablespoon of the vinegar, 3 tablespoons of the olive oil, and a dash of salt. Spread the mixture on a baking sheet and roast for 40 minutes, stirring occasionally. Remove the rosemary and set aside.

Combine the tomato scraps, bay leaf, and 1 cup water in a pot and bring to a boil over high heat. Decrease the heat and simmer, uncovered, for 15 minutes. Strain the stock into a bowl and discard the solids. Rinse the pot and return the stock to the pot. Add the roasted tomatoes. Bring to a boil over high heat, then decrease the heat and simmer, uncovered, for 5 minutes.

Let the soup cool for 10 minutes, then pour into a blender. Add the cheese and blend until smooth. With the blender running, add the remaining 1 tablespoon olive oil. Season to taste with salt.

Garnish the soup with the remaining 1 tablespoon balsamic vinegar and a few grinds of pepper and serve.

Pan-Roasted Portobello Mushrooms with Mashed Parsnips

This savory mushroom dish is the vegetarian equivalent of a steak dinner. The rich taste and dense texture of the portobellos are complemented by creamy parsnips and lightly cooked greens. Serves 4

¼ cup soy sauce	4 portobello mushrooms, stems removed
2 tablespoons balsamic vinegar	2 parsnips, peeled, inner core removed, and coarsely chopped
1 tablespoon honey	
4 tablespoons Tamarind Ketchup (page 178) or regular ketchup	2 Yukon Gold potatoes, peeled and coarsely chopped
2 cloves garlic, smashed	Salt and freshly ground black pepper
5 tablespoons sherry	4 tablespoons minced fresh flat-leaf parsley leaves
8 tablespoons olive oil	1 recipe Sautéed Leafy Greens (page 186)

Preheat the oven to 400°F.

In a blender, combine the soy sauce, vinegar, honey, ketchup, garlic, 3 tablespoons of the sherry, and 3 tablespoons of the olive oil and blend until smooth. Spread the mushrooms on a rimmed baking sheet, gill sides up, and pour the marinade over them. Let marinate for 20 minutes.

Combine the parsnips and potatoes in a saucepan with water to cover. Bring to boil over high heat, then lower the heat and simmer, uncovered, until the vegetables are tender, about 6 minutes. Drain and mash with 3 tablespoons of the olive oil. Season with salt, then cover and set aside.

Heat a large ovenproof pan and add the remaining 2 tablespoons olive oil. Lift the mushrooms out of the marinade, and reserve the marinade for later. Sear the mushrooms, gill side up, for 1 minute. Sear the second sides for 30 seconds and turn off the heat. If the pan isn't big enough, you may need to sear the mushrooms in batches, but it's okay to crowd them in a little for roasting. When you're done searing, pour 1 tablespoon of the reserved marinade over each mushroom and season with salt. Cover and roast in the oven for 20 minutes. Uncover and roast for 5 minutes more.

Transfer the mushrooms to a plate using a slotted spoon. Put the ovenproof pan with the roasting juices back on the stove over high heat, add the reserved marinade and the remaining sherry, and bring to a boil. Reduce the sauce for 1 minute.

To serve, put a scoop of mashed parsnips and potatoes on a plate. Slice the mushrooms in half and put 2 halves on top of the parsnips. Spoon the sauce over the vegetables and garnish with parsley and black pepper. Serve with the sautéed greens.

Roasted Fennel Stuffed with White Beans and Chestnuts

This is a festive entrée for a holiday dinner. The aromatic vegetable stock is made right in the baking dish as the fennel cooks, and then turned into a rich sauce. The trick to carving out the fennel bulbs is to leave the sturdy outer layers intact, no less than ¹/₂ inch thick, or the bulbs can fall apart. If you like, you can mince half of the fennel scraps and add them to the filling. If you can't find chestnuts, substitute toasted walnuts. Serve with a light, fluffy grain like rice or quinoa. **Serves 4**

4 large fennel bulbs, stalks removed

Salt and freshly ground black pepper

¹/₂ cup olive oil, plus more for brushing

1 yellow onion, finely diced, peels and trimmings reserved for stock

3 cloves garlic, minced, peels and trimmings reserved for stock

10 cremini mushrooms, quartered and stems reserved for stock

¹/₂ cup fresh or frozen cranberries

1 cup cooked chestnuts, coarsely chopped to the size of the beans

1 tablespoon dried thyme

¹/₂ teaspoon cayenne pepper

³/₄ cup white wine

1 cup cooked white beans

5 juniper berries

2 dried bay leaves

4 teaspoons unsalted butter

Preheat the oven to 450°F.

To carve out the core of the fennel bulbs, draw a circle with a paring knife on the cut side of the bulb, no less than half an inch from the edge. Carve an **X** through the middle of the circle, and roughly cut out each section of the **X** with the knife. Scrape out the remaining fennel with a melon baller and discard. Rub the fennel bulbs inside and out with salt, pepper, and 1 tablespoon of the olive oil. Place them in a baking dish with a splash of water. Cover and roast for 25 minutes, until slightly tender.

Meanwhile, heat a sauté pan over medium heat and add the remaining 7 tablespoons olive oil. Add the onion and cook until lightly browned, about 5 minutes. Add the garlic, creminis, cranberries, chestnuts, thyme, and cayenne. Add ¹/₄ cup of the wine and ¹/₄ cup water. Bring to a boil, then decrease the heat and simmer, covered, for 10 minutes. Remove the lid and simmer for 10 minutes more.

Decrease the oven heat to 425°F. Fill the fennel bulbs with the beans and put them in the baking dish, then brush the tops with olive oil. Spread the reserved onion, garlic, and mushroom scraps, the juniper berries, and bay leaves between the bulbs. Pour in the remaining $1/2$ cup wine and $1/4$ cup water and roast, uncovered, for 20 minutes. The tops of the fennel should be lightly browned. Transfer the fennel to a platter. Strain the roasting liquid into a bowl and whisk in the butter to make a sauce.

To serve, pour the sauce over the fennel and season with black pepper.

Grape and Ginger–Glazed Chicken

Fresh local grapes are an uncelebrated fall fruit, mostly because of their chewy skin and intrusive seeds. But grapes that aren't ideal for snacking can be more fragrant and sweet than table grapes, and their acidity balances pleasingly with rich roasted chicken. Choose from any white, green, or red variety that's native to your region. Depending on their sweetness, adjust the amount of honey in the recipe. You may use bottled, unsweetened white grape juice instead of fresh grapes. For a comforting cold-weather meal, serve with Watercress Mashed Potatoes (page 185) and Sweet Potato and Cranberry Cornmeal Biscuits (page 189).

Serves 4 to 6

One 2- to 3-pound pasture-raised organic chicken, fat and giblets removed

Kosher salt and freshly ground black pepper

1 head garlic, halved crosswise

4 cups white, green, or red grapes, or 1¹/₂ cups unsweetened white grape juice

1¹/₂ tablespoons minced fresh ginger

1 tablespoon honey

1¹/₂ tablespoons mustard

1 tablespoon unsalted butter

Remove the chicken from the refrigerator an hour before roasting. Rinse the chicken and dry it very well with paper towels, inside and out, to prevent steaming. Season the cavity with 1 teaspoon salt and ¹/₄ teaspoon pepper. Rub the outside with the halved garlic, then stuff it inside the cavity. Tie the legs together with kitchen twine, and tuck the wing tips behind the shoulders. Sprinkle the outside with a mixture of 1¹/₂ tablespoons salt and 1 teaspoon pepper.

Preheat the oven to 450°F.

If using fresh grapes, put the grapes in a food processor. Add the ginger and process for 1 minute. If using bottled juice, put the juice in a blender with the ginger and blend for 30 seconds. Strain the juice into a bowl. Add the honey and mustard and whisk. Set aside.

Place the chicken, breast side up, in a lightly greased ovenproof sauté pan or roasting pan. Roast until the chicken is golden brown and the internal temperature is 165°F, 50 to 70 minutes depending on the size of the bird.

Remove the pan from the oven and tilt the chicken so the juices from the cavity run into the pan. Transfer the chicken to a platter and baste it with the cooking juices. Drizzle 2 tablespoons of the grape juice over the chicken, and let it rest for 15 minutes.

Drain the fat from the roasting pan. Pour in the remaining grape juice and deglaze over low heat, using a wooden spoon to loosen the browned bits from the pan. Turn up the heat and bring the sauce to a boil, then decrease the heat to medium-high and boil gently, uncovered, until the sauce has thickened slightly and reduced to roughly 1 cup, 5 to 7 minutes. Turn off the heat and stir in the butter. Untruss the legs and brush the glaze all over the chicken. Pour the rest in a bowl. Serve immediately with the remaining sauce on the side.

Chicken: Eating Less While Using More

It's generally more economical and environmentally sustainable to buy a whole chicken instead of buying it in parts. The cost per pound of a whole chicken is often a quarter of the price for the breasts alone, and buying a whole chicken cuts down on packaging as well as on the fossil fuels involved in processing. Studies show that livestock production is one of the main culprits responsible for global warming, and experts agree that if we all cut down our consumption of animal products, including poultry, we would dramatically reduce pollution.

If meat weren't so convenient to buy and prepare, we would likely eat much less of it. Roasting a whole chicken takes a little planning, as you'll need to be around for at least the hour it takes to cook. But you'll end up with plenty of food to work with, and you can even make your own soup stock to use in meals for the rest of the week. The act of roasting a whole bird is an event worthy of gathering people together. They will appreciate the food much more than a quick chicken dinner tossed on the stove. What's more, the quality and flavor will be far superior.

Persian Stuffed Dumpling Squash with Rose Petals

This dish features aromatic ingredients used in Persian cuisine; barberries and tart cherries are both sweet and sour, the defining flavors of Persian foods. Find these ingredients at the ethnic food sellers listed in the Resources section (page 193), or substitute more dried apricots for the barberries and dried cranberries for the cherries. The dried rose petals give this dish its distinct floral taste and stunning appearance. Find them at gourmet and Middle Eastern food stores, or dry your own on a screen. Serve with Green Rice (page 190) and Cucumber Yogurt (page 184). **Serves 6**

6 sweet dumpling squash (or substitute acorn squash, or use bell peppers instead)

$^1/_3$ cup olive oil

Salt and freshly ground black pepper

1 large yellow onion, diced

2 cloves garlic, minced

1 cup cooked basmati rice or barley

1 cup walnuts, finely chopped

$^1/_4$ cup barberries

$^1/_2$ cup dried, pitted tart cherries, coarsely chopped

$^1/_4$ cup dried apricots, minced

3 tablespoons dried rose petals, plus more for garnish

$^3/_4$ cup freshly squeezed orange juice

1 teaspoon saffron dissolved in 2 tablespoons hot water

Preheat the oven to 425°F.

Neatly slice off the top of each squash and set it aside. Check the bottoms to see if they're level. If not, slice off enough so that they will stand steadily. Scoop out the seeds and place the squash in an oiled baking dish. Rub them inside and out with olive oil until well coated, and season with salt and pepper.

Heat a skillet over medium heat and add 4 tablespoons of the olive oil, followed by the onion and sauté until lightly browned. Add the garlic, rice, walnuts, barberries, cherries, apricots, and rose petals. Stir well and continue cooking for 5 minutes, adding a little water if the mixture is dry. Taste and season with salt and pepper.

Fill each squash with stuffing and replace the tops. Whisk together the orange juice, saffron water, and the remaining oil and pour over the squash. Cover tightly with a dish lid and bake for 25 minutes, basting occasionally with the juice. Uncover, baste, and bake until the squash is golden and tender, about 5 minutes more.

To serve, transfer the squash to a platter and pour the liquid from the baking dish on top. Garnish with rose petals.

Charred Eggplant and Polenta Torta

I love the smoky flavor of eggplants charred on the stovetop. A "quick and dirty" technique used in restaurants, cooking eggplants on an open flame gets a little messy, but it's fast. This savory pie is made with traditional Italian ingredients and brightened with fresh herbs. Slice it into wedges and serve as a main course, or cut it into small squares for an appetizer. Serve with a simple green salad and fresh bread. **Serves 4**

1 medium-sized globe eggplant

2 tablespoons olive oil, plus extra

Salt and freshly ground black pepper

$^3/_4$ cup instant polenta

2 tomatoes, diced

3 cloves garlic, minced

$^1/_2$ cup vegetable stock

2 tablespoons fresh thyme leaves

2 cups firmly packed fresh spinach leaves, coarsely chopped

1 cup firmly packed fresh basil leaves, torn

4 ounces fontina cheese, coarsely shaved

Turn a gas burner on high and use tongs to place the eggplant directly on the burner. Char the eggplant, turning it once every minute or so, until it is evenly charred, black, and tender, about 6 minutes. Remove from the flame and let cool in a strainer or colander set over a bowl. If you don't have a gas stove, poke holes in the eggplant with a fork and cook on a greased baking sheet in a 400°F oven until soft, 30 to 40 minutes. Let cool. Pull off the charred skin and slice off the stem and discard. Coarsely chop the eggplant flesh and set aside.

Lightly grease a 9-inch round pie dish or a 9 by 13-inch baking sheet with oil. Combine 2$^1/_2$ cups water in a pot with 2 teaspoons salt and bring to a boil. Sprinkle in the polenta and immediately whisk to break up any clumps. Decrease the heat to low and cook for 2 minutes, stirring constantly with a wooden spoon to prevent sticking. Turn off the heat and scrape the hot polenta into the pie dish. Use a wet spatula to smooth the top and set aside.

Preheat the oven to 450°F.

Heat a sauté pan over medium heat and add the 2 tablespoons oil. Add the tomatoes and cook for 1 minute. Add the garlic and eggplant and sauté for 3 minutes, breaking up the eggplant into small pieces with a wooden spoon. Season to taste with salt. Add the stock and bring to a boil.

Decrease the heat and simmer, uncovered, until the liquid has mostly evaporated, about 10 minutes. Stir in the thyme, then stir in the spinach and basil until just wilted. Pour the eggplant mixture over the pan of polenta and smooth the top with a spatula. Spread the cheese evenly over the eggplant and roast in the oven until the cheese is melted and golden, about 12 minutes. Slice and serve.

Black Walnut Tea Cake

Foragers prize black walnuts for their rich taste. Scientists study them because they contain the compound limonene, believed to have anti-cancer properties. Remarkably, one botanist has suggested that limonene inhaled from black walnut trees could help prevent cancer. Removing the hull and extracting the meat is challenging; crushing the nuts under a car tire is a popular method. If you can't find the real thing, use regular walnuts instead. Enjoy this mildly sweet cake with tea or coffee. **Serves 6 to 8**

1 cup unsalted butter, at room temperature	1 tablespoon finely ground coffee beans, sifted
$1/2$ cup plus 1 tablespoon honey	2 teaspoons baking powder
2 eggs	1 teaspoon ground cinnamon
2 cups black walnuts (or regular walnuts), pulsed in a food processor until coarsely ground	$1/4$ teaspoon ground nutmeg
	$1/2$ teaspoon salt
2 cups flour, sifted	2 teaspoons vanilla extract
	2 teaspoons freshly squeezed lemon juice

Preheat the oven to 350°F. Grease a 9-inch round cake pan and cover the bottom with a piece of parchment, or lightly dust with flour.

Combine the butter and honey in the bowl of a mixer and beat until soft and fluffy. Add 1 egg and beat for 1 minute, then repeat with the second egg.

In a large bowl, mix together the walnuts, flour, coffee, baking powder, cinnamon, nutmeg, and salt. Fold the dry mixture into the wet in 3 batches. Stir in the vanilla extract and lemon juice. The finished batter will be quite thick. Scrape the batter into the cake pan and smooth the top with a spatula. Bake for 20 minutes. Rotate the pan and continue baking until a toothpick inserted into the center comes out dry, another 5 to 10 minutes. Let cool. Serve the cake at room temperature.

Fall Fruit Focaccia

Choose your favorite fall fruit to adorn this sweet focaccia. The great Italian cook who taught me how to make it recommended throwing three tablespoons of water into the lower part of the oven (below the pan of focaccia) three times during the first ten minutes of baking. The steam created results in a crispier crust. Try it, but be careful not to extinguish the pilot light or soak the focaccia! Serves 6 to 8

2 tablespoons fresh yeast, or 2 teaspoons active dry yeast

1 tablespoon organic white sugar

5 teaspoons salt

5 cups flour, plus more for kneading

1/4 cup olive oil, plus more as needed

1 cup honey, plus more for serving

3 cups sliced ripe fall fruit, such as figs, plums, seedless grapes, peeled apples, or peeled pears

1/4 cup barley malt syrup (see page 68)

Fresh ricotta for serving (optional)

Crumble the yeast in a small bowl. Add 1/2 cup warm water and the sugar and stir with your fingers until the yeast is dissolved. Set the bowl in a warm place until the yeast starts to foam and bubble, about 5 minutes. Don't let the yeast develop for more than 10 minutes, or it can become inactive.

In a large bowl, stir 4 teaspoons salt into the flour. Make a hole in the middle of the flour and pour in the yeast mixture, 3/4 cup water, the 1/4 cup olive oil, and 1/2 cup of the honey. Coat your hands with olive oil and mix until you have a uniform dough.

Turn the dough onto a floured board and knead for 5 minutes, then transfer the dough to a bowl and drizzle with olive oil. Cover with a damp cloth and put the bowl in a warm place until the dough doubles in size, 60 to 80 minutes.

Oil a 17 by 12-inch rimmed baking sheet and coat your hands with olive oil. Turn the dough onto the baking sheet and press it out to the edges. Make dimples with your fingers all over the dough. (The dimpling helps to hold the honey and barley malt.) Press in the fruit. Cover the pan with a damp cloth and return to a warm place to rise again for 45 minutes.

Preheat the oven to 425°F. Combine the remaining 1/2 cup honey with the barley malt in a small saucepan and bring to a simmer over low heat. Press the dough back out to the edges of the pan if it has shrunk. Brush the warm honey mixture over the fruit and dough and sprinkle with 1 teaspoon salt. Bake the focaccia for 15 minutes. Rotate the pan and bake until the top is firm and golden, about 10 minutes.

Serve warm with ricotta and honey if desired. The focaccia is best eaten the day it is made.

Bittersweet Chocolate Cake
with Prune Purée and Hazelnuts

After my company catered a party spotlighting foods from the state of Oregon, we were left with several pounds of fresh hazelnuts from the Willamette Valley, the capital of U.S. hazelnut production. We added the nuts to a flourless chocolate cake, and the result was this dark, rich confection with fruity undertones. Maple sugar, which is simply dehydrated maple syrup, is sold at most health food stores, but you may substitute any dry sugar. Serve this cake with vanilla-spiked whipped cream. **Serves 8 to 10**

1 cup pitted prunes, soaked in 1 cup water overnight

1 teaspoon vanilla extract

6 ounces semisweet chocolate

$1/2$ cup unsalted butter, at room temperature

1 cup hazelnuts, toasted, peeled, and pulsed in a food processor until coarsely ground

5 eggs, separated

1 cup maple sugar (see page 69)

$1/4$ teaspoon salt

Preheat the oven to 350°F.

Drain the prunes and put them in the bowl of a food processor. Add the vanilla extract and purée until smooth. Set aside.

Grease a 10-inch round cake pan or an 8 by 11-inch baking dish and line it with parchment paper. Grease the paper.

Place the chocolate in a heatproof bowl, then place the bowl on top of a saucepan of simmering water. Melt the chocolate, stirring occasionally.

When the chocolate has melted, remove it from the heat, stir in the butter, and fold in the prune purée and the hazelnuts.

Using a mixer, beat the egg yolks and the maple sugar for 4 minutes, then fold into the chocolate mixture. Using a clean whisk, beat the egg whites with the salt until they hold stiff peaks. Fold the egg whites into the chocolate mixture in 3 batches.

Pour the batter into the prepared pan and smooth the top. Bake for 20 minutes, rotate the pan, and continue baking for 5 to 7 minutes more. The center should still feel slightly soft. Let cool and serve at room temperature. The cake will keep for a couple of days at room temperature, lightly covered with parchment paper.

winter

The cold weather months get a bad rap when it comes to eating seasonally, but in truth, items of rare beauty pass through the market this time of year: Citrus fruits like tiny kumquats and rosy pink grapefruit are juicy and abundant; fruits with a whiff of exotic mystery like pomegranates and quince are an everyday appearance; and hearty cold weather vegetables like red kuri squash, gold beets, and celery root take center stage. In this chapter, you'll find surprising and beautiful ways to prepare all of these, along with winter standouts like Dungeness crab and old-school favorites like apples and pears.

Nothing warms a cold kitchen like a sweet treat baking in the oven, and sharing a homemade dessert over the holidays feels warm and celebratory. Here, you'll learn about sweeteners like barley malt and maple sugar and why they're a better choice for the planet than white sugar. In winter, we crave extra calories, and that usually means more animal products. We'll look at the environmental effects of eating animals and how meat eaters can stay true to their environmental ideals by making adjustments in their diets and shopping habits.

Earth-Friendly Alternatives to White Sugar

It's widely acknowledged that we eat too much processed sugar, and that it plays a major role in such health problems as diabetes, obesity, and attention deficit disorder. What's not as well known are the environmental consequences of our love affair with white sugar.

The harmful practices of sugar production include the discharge of polluted wastewater, the high use of pesticides, and the clearing of wilderness to build plantations. Toxic chemical runoff from sugar plantations threatens the coral of Australia's Great Barrier Reef, and sugar production in the Florida Everglades is largely responsible for the destruction of native plants.

It may take a while for sugar industry practices to catch up with our green expectations. In the meantime, here are some sweeteners with unique flavors and properties that are produced without depleting the earth. Try using these in combination with processed sugar or on their own to make delicious desserts that you can eat in good conscience.

A note on using liquid sweeteners: It's easier to measure them if you grease the measuring cup or spoon. Or, if oil or butter is called for in the recipe, measure those first, and then use the same cup for the sweetener. To loosen up a thick sweetener, place the bottle on a warm spot on the stove, or pour the liquid into a small pot and heat it briefly over a low flame.

BARLEY MALT SYRUP

This sweetener made from fermented barley is thick and dark, with a mineral-like taste. It is delicious baked into bread and is a traditional ingredient in bagels, giving them their unique flavor and crust color. Use it in place of molasses in gingerbread or spice cakes.

Best use: Baked into bread, gingerbread cake, and gingersnaps; cooked into baked beans.

BROWN RICE SYRUP

This caramel-like syrup is made from fermented brown rice. It has a butterscotch flavor that is not overly sweet. In baked goods it produces a crispy texture, so use it in granola or crisp cookies. It can replace corn syrup in desserts like pecan pie.

Best use: Over pancakes; tossed with fresh fruit; baked in cookies, crunch topping, or granola; in gooey dessert fillings.

DRIED FRUIT PURÉE

Delicious purée can be made from any dried fruit. To soften the fruit, simply place 2 cups of dried fruit in a bowl and add 2 cups of boiling water. Cover with a plate and soak for an hour. You can also soak the fruit in room-temperature water overnight in the refrigerator. Strain out the water and purée the fruit in a food processor.

Best use: Baked into cakes; as a fruit filling in desserts like hamantash pastry, or spread between cake layers; as an accompaniment to a cheese platter.

FRUIT JUICE

Many juices, such as orange, apple, and prune, are naturally sweet. Buy juices ready-made, or press your own using a juicing machine. Juice is a superior ingredient in cocktails like sangria, where it asserts its unique character, and from childhood we know that juice frozen in ice trays makes for a perfect popsicle—no sugar added.

Best use: As a sweetener in cocktails; as a poaching liquid for fruit; in pancake batter, salad dressing, and grill marinade.

HONEY

Honey is a potent sweetener whose flavor is determined by which plants the honeybees pollinate, so that it exhibits *terroir*, or regional distinctiveness, just as wine does. Honey made by bees that pollinated orange blossoms in Florida has a different texture, flavor, and color than honey from bees that went to alfalfa flowers in Utah, or sage blossoms in California.

Best use: In all baked goods; over yogurt; on toast with nut butter.

MAPLE SYRUP AND MAPLE SUGAR CRYSTALS

Maple syrup works beautifully as a sweetener in baked desserts and can be dehydrated into crystals for a sweet, dry sugar with a maple taste. Look for maple products from local or organic producers, as large companies have been known to use the chemical paraformaldehyde to make trees "bleed" sap longer. The practice is illegal, but the chemical is still occasionally found in maple products.

Best use: Baked into cakes and cookies; as a topping for pancakes, oatmeal, and yogurt; in marinades and dessert sauces; baked into granola.

ORGANIC DATES

Dates make a satisfying dessert on their own. Date paste is a potent sweetener for cakes and cookies, or can be used as a simple raw confection rolled with nuts and coconut flakes. Date sugar, made from ground dehydrated dates, can be used in place of sugar for baking, although it is not nearly as sweet, and its dark hue can alter the color of food.

Best use: In baking, like any fruit purée or to replace dry sugar; baked into crunch topping for a crumbly texture.

STEVIA

Stevia is a plant whose leaves naturally taste sweet. Simply chew on a leaf for a sweet taste tinged with licorice, or place a fresh leaf in hot water to make tea. The dried leaves are sold as an herbal tea, but stevia is most commonly found in powder or liquid form. Just a pinch of powder or a few drops of the liquid is enough to sweeten a smoothie or a cup of hot chocolate. If you add too much, though, the flavor becomes bitter, so use it sparingly.

Best use: In fresh, powdered, or liquid form as a sweetener in beverages.

Is eating animals bad for the environment? The short answer is yes. The majority of the animal products we eat, including meat, fish, eggs, and dairy, comes from Concentrated Animal Feeding Operations (CAFOs), better known as factory farms. An abundance of environmental problems are linked to CAFOs, including water pollution from waste runoff, methane gas production caused by large concentrations of animal manure, and high pesticide quantities used in growing the grains that feed the animals. (For more on this subject, see the books listed in the section "Making Informed Food Choices," in Resources, page 194.)

In general, the planet would almost certainly be better off if we all became vegetarians. However, it's obvious that the world is not going to go 100 percent vegetarian any time soon.

What can you do in the meantime? Start by making meat a smaller part of your diet, and buy meat and animal products from small local farms. When you buy from small farmers, you reduce the need for factory farms, the culprits of the most tangible environmental damage.

I try to buy all of my animal proteins locally, including wild fish, free-range eggs, and milk from a dairy where I can return the glass bottles for a deposit. In general, small farm practices follow tried-and-true methods of animal husbandry that work in harmony with the

ecosystem, such as feeding cattle their natural diet of grass on rotating tracts of land, eschewing the use of antibiotics, and spending fewer natural resources on transportation by selling to people within 150 miles of their farm. Small farms benefit from healthy surroundings, and most farmers make supportive gestures toward the environment like leaving parts of their land wild to encourage the return of native plants and animals, or planting trees and flowers in strategic spots that encourage the presence of birds, butterflies, bats, and bees.

If I am going to eat or serve meat, or otherwise support the practice of eating animals, I can make an informed choice about whom I pay for those products. Exercised by a critical mass of people, that choice can determine the way animals are treated up to the moment they reach our tables, and in turn have a positive outcome for the environment.

So far I haven't touched upon the question of whether it is morally wrong to kill animals for food, nor what might constitute humane treatment of livestock. One trip to a slaughterhouse or industrialized egg farm is often enough to make people rethink their entire diet. For years I didn't eat meat or animal products because of the inhumane treatment of farm animals, and even today close to 95 percent of my diet consists of produce, grains, and legumes. On a recent trip to

Italy, however, I decided to eat whatever my very generous hosts served, and that included prosciutto, wild boar, and—most problematically for me—veal. Under normal circumstances I wouldn't serve veal myself, and perhaps I'll never eat it again, as I wholly disapprove of the way it's produced. Still, in that instance, it made more sense to me to participate in the social bonding that took place around the dinner table, even though it meant compromising my beliefs, than to sit out the experience with my conscience intact. For me, it feels appropriate to assess eating choices as they arise, based on factors ranging from the social to the environmental.

I urge you to make an informed choice about eating meat and animal products, one that supports your goals for the environment. Visit small animal, dairy, and egg farms; try to view film footage from factory farms (in general, you can't visit them—they are simply too gruesome); and look into the effects of farming on the region in which you live. You may decide to stop eating meat, eat only locally raised animals, or save meat for special occasions.

Apple Pomegranate Sangria

Exotic, jewel-like, and demanding considerable labor to penetrate their maze of pulp, pome-granates are a ravishing winter treat. A constant on the Lucid Food cocktail menu during cold weather, this drink pairs well with food but also stands on its own. You can make the sangria the day before, but wait until the day you serve it to add the orange slices, as the pith can cause the drink to turn bitter. Use a cheap red wine; I prefer a rioja or a tempranillo.
Serves 6

1 (750-ml) bottle dry red wine

4 cups apple juice

1/2 cup brandy

Juice of 1 lime

2 sweet, crisp apples, finely diced

Seeds of 1 large pomegranate

1 orange, halved and sliced into half moons 1/4 inch thick

Sparkling water for serving (optional)

Combine all the ingredients in a pitcher. Refrigerate for a few hours before serving to allow the flavors to marry. If you'd like a little fizz, top off glasses of the sangria with sparkling water.

Nutty Banana Shake

This rich drink makes a filling breakfast. For a superb eggnog, add orange zest and rum, brandy, or bourbon. Before buying bananas, read about their production in "Must-Buy Organics," on page 16. If you like nondairy milk, then blending your own nut milk, as described in this recipe, is much more economical than buying it premade. And unlike store-bought nut milk, it comes without added sugar, preservatives, and hard-to-recycle cartons. Homemade nut milk works beautifully for cereal, smoothies, baking, and simply drinking on its own.
Serves 2 to 4

1 cup almonds, soaked in water for
$^1/_2$ hour, or 3 cups commercially prepared
almond milk

1 banana, peeled and broken into pieces

$^1/_2$ cup smooth almond butter

1 tablespoon vanilla extract

$^1/_2$ teaspoon ground cinnamon

$^1/_4$ teaspoon ground nutmeg

If you are making your own almond milk, drain the almonds, then place them in a blender with 3 cups water and blend until the almonds are completely pulverized, about 1 minute. Pour the milk through a fine-mesh strainer, using a ladle to press the liquid from the almonds. You should end up with 3 cups of almond milk.

Rinse out the blender, then pour in the almond milk. Add all of the remaining ingredients and blend until smooth. Serve at room temperature or chilled. Or, for a colder drink, blend in a few ice cubes and serve immediately.

Green Smoothie

Take a break from cooking and make a satisfying meal from raw fruits and vegetables. This drink takes about twelve minutes to make from start to finish. It's a great way to get your greens without any work, and I like the slightly fibrous texture the greens impart. The smoothie is good for two days if you want to have it for a few meals. After storing it overnight in the refrigerator, just reblend it for a few seconds. As different fruits come into season, try berries instead of oranges, or a ripe peach instead of the banana. In hot weather, blend in several ice cubes. Makes 6 cups

1 cup firmly packed kale, collard, or other leafy greens, stems removed and coarsely chopped

¼ cup loosely packed fresh flat-leaf parsley leaves

1 carrot, peeled and coarsely chopped

1 sweet apple, coarsely chopped

1 large banana, coarsely chopped

2 oranges, peeled and coarsely chopped

¼ cup almonds

2¼ cups water

Place all of the ingredients in a blender and blend until smooth. If the mixture is too thick, add a little more water.

Indian Spiced Scrambled Eggs

The key to this dish is the texture of the eggs—they should be airy and light. For fluffy eggs, take them out of the pan when they are just barely cooked. For a richer dish, use milk instead of water, or add a cup of Cheddar or other mild cheese just before the eggs leave the stove. Serve with Cilantro-Jalapeño Sauce (page 184), Tamarind Ketchup (page 178), or Citrus Chutney (page 182). **Serves 4 to 6**

1 Yukon Gold potato, peeled and diced	1 tablespoon mustard seeds
2 cups cauliflower florets	1 teaspoon ground turmeric
5 tablespoons olive oil	1 teaspoon ground cinnamon
1 yellow onion, diced	1/4 teaspoon cayenne pepper
1 tablespoon ground coriander	Salt
1 tablespoon minced fresh ginger	6 eggs
1 tablespoon ground cumin	

Place the potato in a saucepan with salted water to cover. Bring to a boil over high heat and boil for 4 minutes. Add the cauliflower and boil for 1 minute more. Drain the vegetables.

Heat a skillet over medium-high heat and add 3 tablespoons of the oil. Add the onion, and cook until soft. Add the potato, cauliflower, spices, and a dash of salt. Decrease the heat to medium and sauté for 5 minutes. Turn off the heat, transfer the vegetable mixture to a large bowl, and cover. Return the skillet to the stove.

Crack the eggs into a bowl and add 2 tablespoons water and 3 dashes of salt. Whisk for 2 minutes, tilting the bowl as you whisk to whip as much air into the eggs as possible. Heat the skillet over medium-high heat and add the remaining 2 tablespoons olive oil. When the oil is hot, pour in the eggs. Allow them to begin to set before stirring, then gently push the eggs toward the center of the pan with a wooden spoon. Tilt the pan to evenly distribute the uncooked eggs. When the eggs are just firm, flip them over and cook for 25 seconds more.

Transfer the eggs to the bowl of vegetables and stir to mix. Taste and season with salt. Serve immediately.

Congee with Vegetables and Fresh Herbs

In many parts of the world, breakfast is a savory affair. Throughout Asia, hearty congee is a favorite morning dish, eaten with condiments ranging from stir-fried pork to fried garlic. This version gets a citrus zing from lemongrass (shown below) and ginger. Normally made with white rice, the grain most widely available in Asia, congee can be made using any whole grain. Soaking the rice overnight cuts the cooking time in half. Serves 6

1 cup long-grain brown rice, soaked in 3 cups of water overnight

1 sweet potato, peeled and diced

2 stalks lemongrass, bruised (see page 155)

7 cups vegetable or chicken stock or water

Salt

2 teaspoons minced fresh ginger

2 tablespoons olive oil

1 bunch bok choy, trimmed and finely diced

2 scallions, green and white parts, thinly sliced

1 large handful fresh cilantro leaves

1/2 cup coarsely chopped toasted peanuts or almonds

Soy sauce for serving

Sesame oil for serving

Red pepper flakes for serving

Drain the rice and place it in a large pot with the sweet potato. Cut the lemongrass stalks in half horizontally and add them to the pot. Add the stock and 1 tablespoon salt and bring to a boil. Decrease the heat and simmer, covered, for 35 minutes.

Remove the lid and increase the heat so the rice is bubbling. Remove the lemongrass and discard. Simmer, stirring frequently to prevent it from sticking, until the rice is tender and has the consistency of a thick porridge, about 15 minutes more. Add the ginger in the last 5 minutes of cooking.

Heat a sauté pan over medium-high heat and add the olive oil. Add the bok choy and cook until tender and wilted, about 4 minutes. Season with salt and remove from the heat.

To serve, put the bok choy, scallions, cilantro, and nuts into small bowls. Ladle the porridge into bowls and let diners garnish it with the vegetables, nuts, soy sauce, sesame oil, and red pepper flakes.

Brown Rice: More than Just Healthy

We know that brown rice has more nutrients than white rice, but aside from health concerns, white rice is put through many stages of processing, all requiring fossil fuels and chemicals. First, the germ and bran are removed to extend the length of time the rice can be stored; then synthetic vitamins are added back in; and finally, the rice is polished with water, glucose, or the mineral talc, which is known to cause stomach cancer. The taste of brown rice can take some getting used to, but cooked with fragrant seasonings like the ones in the congee recipe, it can please even the pickiest of palates.

Inarizushi (Stuffed Tofu Pockets)

Pockets made from fried tofu skins are convenient for making a quick finger food for parties, and they don't require any dipping sauce. Find the pockets in Japanese markets in the dry foods or refrigerated section; they come preseasoned with sugar and soy. You'll find kimchi, the sweet and spicy fermented cabbage condiment, at the same store. Although it originated in Korea, kimchi is also very popular in Japan. **Makes 10 pockets**

1 cup sushi rice

2 tablespoons dry sugar, such as maple crystals or organic white sugar

2 tablespoons soy sauce

2 tablespoons rice vinegar

1 tablespoon sesame oil

1 tablespoon olive oil

1/2 cup shiitake mushrooms, thinly sliced

1/2 cup shredded carrots

1/2 cup shredded red cabbage

1/4 cup thinly sliced scallion greens

2 tablespoons prepared kimchi

2 teaspoons minced fresh ginger

Salt

10 square fried tofu pockets

1 tablespoon toasted black sesame seeds

Rinse the rice in cold water and drain. Put the rice in a saucepan with 1 cup water and bring to a boil. Decrease the heat and simmer, covered, until the water is absorbed, about 20 minutes. Turn off the heat and let the rice stand, covered, for 15 minutes. Stir in the sugar, soy sauce, vinegar, and sesame oil. Let cool.

Heat a small sauté pan over medium heat and add the olive oil, followed by the shiitakes. Cook for 3 minutes, stirring frequently, until soft. Let cool.

Combine the shiitakes, carrots, cabbage, scallion greens, kimchi, and ginger in a large bowl. Add the rice and mix everything together. Taste and season with salt.

Open the pockets and push the rice mixture in with your fingers. Stuff them about three-quarters full, so they can stand with the rice facing up, and sprinkle the rice with a few sesame seeds.

Serve the pockets on a platter at room temperature.

Crispy Yuba Rolls with Lime-Mustard Dipping Sauce

Yuba, also called tofu skin, is sturdy and easy to work with. Its crisp texture when baked makes it an ideal wrapper for spring rolls. Find dried or frozen yuba sheets at Japanese food stores. Serves 4 to 6

4 tablespoons olive oil

8 shiitake mushrooms, stems removed and thinly sliced

1 large carrot, julienned

1 large burdock root, peeled and julienned (see page 48)

1 tablespoon minced fresh ginger

1 clove garlic, minced

1 tablespoon maple syrup

1 tablespoon soy sauce

2 tablespoons sesame oil

2 cups firmly packed shredded napa cabbage

Salt

10 sheets yuba, each about 6 by 4 inches, reconstituted according to package directions and drained

SAUCE

2 tablespoons freshly squeezed lime juice

1/2 teaspoon sesame oil

2 tablespoons honey

1/2 teaspoon soy sauce

1 tablespoon Dijon mustard

Salt

Preheat the oven to 400°F. Grease a baking sheet and line it with parchment paper.

Heat 2 tablespoons of the olive oil in a large sauté pan and add the shiitakes. Cook, stirring, for 2 minutes, then add the carrot, burdock root, ginger, garlic, maple syrup, soy sauce, and 1 tablespoon of the sesame oil. Cook for 5 minutes. Add the cabbage and cook for 1 minute more. Remove from the heat and let cool. Transfer the vegetables to a bowl and season with salt.

In a bowl, whisk together the remaining 2 tablespoons olive oil and 1 tablespoon sesame oil. Spread out a sheet of yuba on your work surface. Spread a scant 1/2 cup of the vegetables on the yuba sheet in a line 1 inch wide along the long edge of the sheet. Tightly roll the yuba sheet around the vegetables, as if you were rolling sushi. Place the roll on the prepared baking sheet, seam side down. Repeat with the rest of the filling and yuba sheets. Brush the rolls with the oil mixture and bake until the rolls are crisp and golden, about 15 minutes.

To make the sauce, whisk together all of the ingredients. Season with salt to taste.

Serve the rolls hot, sliced in half on the diagonal, with the dipping sauce.

Grapefruit and Celery Root Salad
with Watercress

Pretty pink grapefruits add zing and color to salads. Supreming citrus fruits (see the pictures on page 97) gives you seed- and rind-free sections that are ready to eat with no fuss, and the process releases a considerable amount of juice, which you'll use as the base of the dressing. Once you have peeled the celery root, soak it in water with a little bit of lemon juice to keep it from turning brown. **Serves 2 to 4**

1 ripe grapefruit, supremed (see page 97)

1 scallion, white part only, minced

3 tablespoons olive oil

1 tablespoon honey

1 tablespoon Dijon mustard

Salt and freshly ground black pepper

$^1/_2$ medium-sized celery root, peeled

1 bunch watercress, coarsely chopped

Small chunk of Grana Padano or Pecorino Romano cheese

Squeeze the juice from the grapefruit membrane into the large bowl. Add the scallion, olive oil, honey, and mustard and whisk together. Season with salt and set aside.

Cut the celery root into matchsticks and add it to the dressing. Toss to coat thoroughly, and let marinate for 1 hour.

To serve, put the watercress in a large bowl. Drain the marinated celery root, reserving the dressing, and add it to the watercress. Add a few tablespoons of the dressing and toss. Season with salt and pepper. Divide the salad among the plates, topping each one with the grapefruit sections. Using a vegetable peeler, shave several thin pieces of Grana Padano over each salad.

Organic Honey: Start Your Own Hive!

In recent years, a fourth of all U.S. honeybees have vanished due to an epidemic dubbed *colony collapse disorder*, the result of pesticide exposure, an inadequate food supply, and a virus that targets bees' immune systems. This phenomenon is worth noting, as bees play a critical role in our food supply by pollinating crops.

One way to help bees is to build a beehive, which makes perfect sense considering the current search for local food solutions. The University of Connecticut, for example, set up ten large hives in the summer of 2008 to supply the four thousand pounds of honey used by the campus dining services each year.

There are many reasons to build your own hive, from teaching children about the process of pollination, to supporting local food production, to helping bee populations thrive. Tending honeybees may be easier than you think: They are gentle creatures that don't sting unless provoked, and most people are not severely allergic to bee stings. If you decide to keep hives, classes or training are essential. Beekeeping communities have regular demonstrations and literature available for those who are interested. Searching online for your local beekeeping community will point you in the direction of resources. For some good websites to help you get started, see the Resources section on page 193.

Cucumber and Pomegranate Salad

The festive colors of this Mediterranean salad brighten a holiday meal, and its light, refreshing character makes it a great counterpoint to hearty winter dishes. It should be served as soon as it's made, or it can turn soggy. You can prepare the individual ingredients ahead of time and store them in separate bowls, tossing everything together just before serving.

Serves 4

2 cucumbers, peeled, halved,
and seeds removed

Seeds of 1 pomegranate

¼ cup thinly sliced scallions,
green parts only

½ cup fresh cilantro leaves

Juice of 1 lime

3 tablespoons olive oil

Salt and freshly ground black pepper

½ cup crumbled feta cheese

Cut the cucumbers into slices ¼ inch thick. Put the cucumber slices in a bowl with all but 4 tablespoons of the pomegranate seeds. Add the scallions, cilantro, lime juice, and olive oil. Toss and season with salt.

To serve, divide the salad among bowls and top with the crumbled feta, a tablespoon of pomegranate seeds, and a few grinds of pepper.

Red Cabbage, Apple, and Dulse Salad

This pretty scarlet salad is enhanced by dulse (shown opposite), a sea vegetable with a rich, meaty taste— try toasted dulse in place of bacon in a DLT! Several eco-friendly companies along the North American Atlantic coast harvest dulse by hand in small boats, dry it outside, and sell it with minimal packaging. When toasting dulse, pass it back and forth a few times over a flame and then let it cool. The texture should be crisp and crackly. If the dulse is still soft, repeat this process until it breaks up easily. Toasting it gently and gradually prevents burning. Serves 2 to 4

2 scallions, green and white parts, minced	1 teaspoon grated fresh ginger
1 tablespoon sweet white miso	1 sweet, crisp apple
1 teaspoon Dijon mustard	1/2 cup whole dulse leaves
1 1/2 tablespoons rice vinegar	2 cups shredded cabbage
3 tablespoons olive oil	Salt

In a large bowl, whisk together the minced scallions, miso, mustard, vinegar, oil, and ginger. Julienne the apple and add the slices to the dressing, tossing lightly to coat. Using scissors, cut 1/4 cup of the dulse into thin strips. Add it to the apples, followed by the cabbage. Toss and season with salt.

Turn a gas burner on medium. Holding the pieces with tongs, quickly pass the remaining dulse leaves over the flame once or twice. They should be lightly toasted with a crackly texture. Break into bite-size pieces.

To serve, divide the salad among the plates and top each with several pieces of toasted dulse.

Creamy Red Kuri Squash Soup

I look forward to seeing the stunning array of brightly colored winter squash that appears at the market every autumn. Of all the varieties, red kuri squash (shown below) is my favorite for savory dishes. It has a rich, full flavor that makes this simple soup exceptional. The soup lasts for several days in the refrigerator. To reheat, add a little stock or water, because it will thicken over time. **Serves 4 to 6**

4 heaping cups coarsely diced squash, seeds removed

1 quart vegetable stock

Salt and freshly ground black pepper

3 tablespoons olive oil

1 yellow onion, sliced

1 sweet apple, cored and sliced

1 teaspoon ground cinnamon

Pinch of cayenne pepper

Place the squash in a soup pot with the stock and a dash of salt and bring to a boil. Simmer, covered, until tender, about 15 minutes. Drain the squash, reserving the stock.

Heat a skillet over high heat and add 2 tablespoons of the olive oil. Add the onion and sauté until it begins to brown. Add the apple, cinnamon, cayenne, and a dash of salt and sauté until the apples are soft and lightly browned.

In batches, if necessary, combine the squash, onion, apple, and stock in a blender. Purée until smooth, adding the remaining tablespoon of olive oil as it blends. Add a little extra stock or water if the soup is too thick. Taste and season with salt.

Serve hot with a few grinds of black pepper.

Warming Asian Rutabaga Soup

Rutabagas are a robust winter standby that lend themselves well to Asian dishes, where they can act as a sweeter stand-in for the turnips often used in Chinese, Japanese, and Korean cooking. I use chicken stock in this recipe because its richness brings all of the subtle flavors of the dish alive. The star anise lends this soup a fragrant, smoky sweetness. **Serves 4**

4 scallions, green and white parts separated

5 tablespoons olive oil

2 cloves garlic, minced

3 cups rutabaga, peeled and diced

$1/2$ teaspoon ground white pepper

2 star anise

3 tablespoons soy sauce

4 cups chicken stock

Salt

16 ounces extra firm tofu, drained and diced

2 cups shiitake mushrooms, loosely packed and diced

1 tablespoon fresh ginger, minced

Sesame oil for serving

Chile flakes for serving

Rice vinegar or apple cider vinegar for serving

Fresh cilantro leaves for serving

Thinly slice the scallion greens and set them aside. Mince the scallion whites.

Heat a soup pot over medium-high heat and add 2 tablespoons of the olive oil. Add the scallion whites and garlic and sauté for 1 minute. Add the rutabaga, white pepper, star anise, and 2 tablespoons of the soy sauce and cook, stirring, for 1 minute. Pour in the stock and bring to a boil. Decrease the heat and simmer, covered, until the rutabaga is tender, about 20 minutes. Taste and season with salt.

Heat a sauté pan over medium heat and add the remaining 3 tablespoons of olive oil. Add the tofu and spread it evenly across the pan. Fry for 2 minutes, undisturbed. Season with salt. Flip the tofu and cook for 1 minute more. Add the shiitakes, ginger, and the remaining tablespoon of soy sauce and cook for 2 minutes, then remove from the heat.

To serve, ladle into bowls and add $1/2$ cup of the tofu mixture to each bowl. Garnish with a few drops of sesame oil, chile flakes to taste, a dash of vinegar, and a generous amount of the scallion greens and cilantro leaves.

Fesenjan (Chicken in Pomegranate Walnut Sauce)

Fesenjan combines fruit and meat, a Persian cooking style that traveled to Europe in the Middle Ages. This version gets its deep ruby color from the addition of beets (shown opposite). Served with rice, this stew makes for a sumptuous feast. Instead of chicken, try using duck or tempeh. Look for pomegranate syrup at natural and Middle Eastern food stores. If you can't find pomegranate syrup, substitute 2½ cups of unsweetened pomegranate juice and leave out the stock. **Serves 6**

4 tablespoons olive oil

2 pounds skinless chicken legs or breasts, rinsed and patted dry

1 large or 2 small yellow onions, diced

2 beets, peeled, quartered, and sliced ¼ inch thick

1½ cups walnuts, pulsed in a food processor until coarsely ground

1 clove garlic, minced

1 teaspoon ground cinnamon

Pinch of cayenne pepper

½ cup unsweetened pomegranate syrup

Salt

2 cups vegetable or chicken stock

1 recipe Green Rice (page 190)

Seeds from ½ pomegranate

Fresh cilantro leaves for garnish

2 recipes Cucumber Yogurt (page 184)

Heat a skillet over high heat and add 2 tablespoons of the olive oil. When the oil is hot, add the chicken and brown lightly on both sides, working in batches to avoid crowding the pan. Remove the pan from the heat and set aside.

Heat a large sauté pan over medium-high heat and add the remaining 2 tablespoons olive oil. Add the onions and cook until lightly browned. Add the beets, walnuts, garlic, cinnamon, and cayenne and cook, stirring, for 1 minute. Add the pomegranate syrup and stock and bring to a boil. Cook at a low boil, covered, for 10 minutes.

Add the chicken and simmer, uncovered and stirring occasionally, for 30 minutes. The stew should be bubbling the whole time. Turn the chicken pieces over every 10 to 15 minutes. Taste and add salt, if necessary. The beets should be fork-tender.

To serve, transfer the chicken to a cutting board. For chicken legs, separate the thigh from the drumstick. For breasts, slice each one into 2 or 3 pieces. Put a small mound of rice on each plate with a few pieces of chicken on top. Spoon the stew over the chicken. Sprinkle the pomegranate seeds and several cilantro leaves on top. Serve the cucumber yogurt on the side.

Mediterranean Shepherd's Pie

This rustic dish makes a wonderful cold-weather meal when paired with a green salad. Instead of the usual white top made of potatoes, this shepherd's pie gets a toasted orange hue from winter squash, a common ingredient in Greek and Italian cuisine. You can substitute pumpkin, red kuri squash, or kabocha squash for the butternut. Gremolata, a fresh Italian condiment of parsley, lemon zest, and garlic, adds a bright citrus note. Serves 6 to 8

5 cups peeled and diced butternut squash (roughly a $1/2$-pound squash)

Salt and freshly ground black pepper

6 tablespoons olive oil

1 yellow onion, diced

2 cups fresh leafy greens, stemmed and finely chopped

2 cloves garlic, minced, plus 1 clove peeled and smashed

2 cups cooked chickpeas or 1 (15-ounce) can chickpeas, drained and rinsed

1 cup walnuts, pulsed in a food processor until coarsely ground

5 anchovy fillets, minced

$1^1/_2$ cups vegetable or chicken stock

$1/2$ cup bread crumbs

1 cup fresh flat-leaf parsley leaves

Zest of 1 lemon

Preheat the oven to 400°F.

Toss the squash with salt and pepper and 3 tablespoons of the olive oil. Arrange it in a single layer on a baking sheet and roast until the squash is very soft, about 50 minutes. Stir occasionally. Let the squash cool and purée it in a food processor until smooth. Season with salt and set aside.

Heat a large sauté pan over medium-high heat and add 2 tablespoons olive oil. Add the onion and sauté until soft. Add the greens and cook for 2 minutes. Stir in the minced garlic, chickpeas, walnuts, and anchovies. Add the stock and bring to a boil. Decrease the heat and simmer, uncovered, for 15 minutes.

Transfer the chickpea mixture to a 10-inch round glass baking dish, and spread the squash purée evenly over the top. Sprinkle the bread crumbs over the squash in a thin layer, then drizzle with the 1 remaining tablespoon olive oil. Bake until the bread crumbs are lightly browned, 20 to 25 minutes.

To make the gremolata, combine the parsley, zest, and smashed garlic clove in a food processor, and grind to a coarse meal. Set aside in a small dish. Serve the pie in slices with the gremolata scattered on top.

Lemony Gold Beet Barley Risotto

Barley replaces the traditional Arborio rice here for a textured, nutty-tasting whole-grain risotto. Soaking the barley overnight reduces its cooking time. Gold beets have a sweet, mellow flavor. When roasted with the skin intact, their beautiful color is preserved. Wait to salt the risotto until you've added the ricotta salata; as the name implies, it is quite salty. This aged ricotta does not melt, but instead retains a pleasant firm chewiness. **Serves 6**

2 gold beets	1 yellow onion, finely diced
2 teaspoons lemon zest	1 cup pearled barley, soaked in water overnight in the refrigerator
1 tablespoon plus 1 teaspoon freshly squeezed lemon juice	2 cloves garlic, minced
6 tablespoons olive oil, plus more for serving	1 cup white wine
	$1^1/_4$ cups crumbled ricotta salata
Salt and freshly ground black pepper	2 recipes Sautéed Leafy Greens (page 186)
4 cups vegetable or chicken stock	

Preheat the oven to 400°F.

Wash and trim the beets, leaving a little of the stems intact so that you do not cut into the beets themselves. Wash the beet leaves and add them to the leafy greens for sautéing. Put the beets in a casserole dish with 3 tablespoons water. Cover tightly and roast until the beets are very tender, about 45 minutes. When cool, pull off and discard the skins and coarsely chop the beets. Put the beets in a bowl and mash them coarsely. Add the zest, lemon juice, 3 tablespoons of the olive oil, and a dash of salt. Mix well and set aside.

Pour the stock into a pot and bring to a boil. Decrease the heat to a simmer.

Heat a large soup pot over medium-high heat. Add the remaining 3 tablespoons olive oil, then the onion, and sauté until translucent, about 5 minutes. Remove the barley from the soaking water, then add the barley and garlic to the soup pot and sauté for 1 minute. Stir in the wine and cook until it has evaporated, about 2 minutes. Ladle a cup of stock into the risotto and stir until the liquid is absorbed. Repeat, adding the stock 1 cup at a time, until the barley is tender. This will take about 30 minutes. Reserve $^1/_4$ cup of the stock to stir into the risotto at the very end.

When the barley is tender, stir in all but a few tablespoons of the beets and cook for 1 minute. Turn off the heat and fold in 1 cup of the ricotta and the remaining $^1/_4$ cup stock.

To serve, put a cup of risotto on each plate and spoon a little olive oil on top. Top with the remaining ricotta and the reserved diced beets. Serve with the leafy greens, seasoning with pepper.

Oven-Roasted Dungeness Crab with Fennel and Orange

This dish is inspired by the Provençal ingredients of fennel, orange, and fresh seafood. For the fullest flavor, rub the marinade into all the cracks and crevices of the crab shell. You'll want to have bibs, nutcrackers, and crab forks on hand to enjoy this meal in all of its messy goodness. Serve with a light green salad and plenty of fresh, crusty bread to soak up the sauce. **Serves 4**

3 cloves garlic, minced

$^1/_2$ cup olive oil

$^1/_4$ cup Dijon mustard

1 orange, zested and supremed (see page 97)

15 sprigs fresh thyme

2 Dungeness crabs, cooked, cleaned, cracked, and split in half

1 shallot, thinly sliced

1 fennel bulb, trimmed and thinly sliced

1$^1/_2$ cups dry white wine

$^1/_2$ cup freshly squeezed orange juice

Salt and freshly ground black pepper

1 carrot, peeled and sliced on the diagonal

1 large handful fingerling potatoes, halved

$^1/_4$ cup unsalted butter

1 lemon, quartered

continued on page 96

Sustainable Seafood Choice: Dungeness Crab

A winter treat to look forward to, Dungeness crab is a sustainable seafood choice because Dungeness fisheries are so well run: Only male crabs at least 6$^1/_4$ inches long are caught and sold, allowing them 1 to 2 years to mate as adults; traps let undersized crabs escape, and females are returned to the water; and fishing gear made from biodegradable webs prevents "ghost fishing," when traps abandoned underwater trap animals indefinitely. Over the last fifty years these fishing practices have helped to preserve a thriving Dungeness population.

Whisk together the garlic, 6 tablespoons of the olive oil, the mustard, and orange zest. Toss in 10 of the thyme sprigs. Place the crabs in a shallow baking dish and smear the garlic mixture all over them, working it into the cracks in the shell. Set aside in the refrigerator.

Preheat the oven to 425°F.

Heat a large ovenproof sauté pan over medium-high heat and add the remaining 2 tablespoons olive oil. Add the shallot and sauté for 1 minute. Add the fennel and the rest of the thyme and sauté for 1 minute. Pour in the wine and orange juice and bring to a boil. Add salt to taste, decrease the heat, and simmer for 5 minutes. Add the carrot and potatoes and simmer, covered, until the vegetables are cooked through, about 20 minutes.

Add the crab and all of the marinade to the pan and bring to a boil. Taste the sauce and season as needed. Cover the pan and put it in the oven for 5 minutes. Baste the crab with the sauce and roast for 5 minutes more. Take the pan out of the oven and carefully pour the sauce through a large strainer into a bowl. Cover the crab to keep it warm.

Pour the sauce into a small saucepan and bring it to a boil. Reduce the sauce, stirring often, for 4 minutes. Turn off the heat and whisk in the butter. To serve, divide the crab and vegetables among the plates. Pour the sauce over the crab and season with pepper. Garnish with orange supremes and a lemon quarter.

Citrus Fruit Supremes

To supreme an orange or grapefruit, use a very sharp knife to slice the peel from the top and bottom of the fruit. Place the fruit on one of its flat surfaces and slice down, following the curve of the fruit, to remove the pith, leaving no white spots clinging to the flesh. Working over a large bowl to catch the juice as you cut, line your knife up along one of the membranes separating one section from another, and make an incision from the outside of the fruit to its center. Move your knife to the membrane on the other side of that section, and make another cut. The wedge of fruit should fall out. If it doesn't, go back and sever any membrane connecting the section to the fruit. Repeat until you've cut out all of the sections. Lift the sections out of the bowl and store them in the refrigerator.

Buckwheat and Orange Zest Gingersnaps

Orange zest gives these crispy snaps a hint of citrus. Barley malt syrup (for more about this sweetener, see page 68) stands in for the traditional molasses, and tastes virtually identical. If the maple sugar is clumpy, break it up with your fingers before creaming it with the butter. To make gingerbread people, roll the dough to just over 1/4 inch thick and press in raisins or other toppings to decorate the cookies. Makes approximately 40 cookies

1¹⁄₂ cups unsalted butter, at room temperature

1¹⁄₂ cups maple sugar (see page 69), or other dry sugar

1 teaspoon vanilla extract

1 egg

Zest of ¹⁄₂ orange

2 tablespoons grated fresh ginger

¹⁄₂ cup barley malt syrup

1¹⁄₂ cups white flour, plus more for rolling out dough

1¹⁄₂ cups buckwheat flour

2 teaspoons baking soda

¹⁄₂ teaspoon salt

1 tablespoon ground cinnamon

1 teaspoon allspice

¹⁄₂ teaspoon ground cloves

¹⁄₄ teaspoon ground nutmeg

Cream together the butter and maple sugar in the bowl of an electric mixer until light and fluffy. Beat in the vanilla extract, egg, orange zest, and ginger. Add the barley malt and beat until smooth.

In a large bowl, sift together the dry ingredients. With the mixer on low, add the dry ingredients to the butter mixture in batches, ¹⁄₂ cup at a time, mixing just until everything is combined. Transfer the dough to a bowl and store in the refrigerator, covered, for 1 hour.

Preheat the oven to 350°F.

Flour your work surface and line a baking sheet with parchment paper. Take half of the dough from the refrigerator and roll it out to slightly less than ¹⁄₄ inch thick. Cut out the cookies with a 3-inch cookie cutter, and place them on the baking sheet 1 inch apart. Gather the scraps and reroll the dough. If the dough gets too soft, put it back in the refrigerator for a couple of minutes.

Bake the cookies until golden, 8 to 10 minutes. Transfer the cookies to a wire rack and let cool. Repeat with the remaining dough. When cool, store the cookies in an airtight container.

Pear Kanten with Pecan Crunch

A kanten dessert is the Japanese equivalent of Jell-O, and its consistency can be adjusted by adding more or less liquid. This version is soft in texture, and the mellow flavor of pears is set off by the rich, spiced crunch topping. It's important to blend the kanten after it cools in order to achieve a smooth, creamy texture. If you can't find agar-agar (see page 102) in powder form, simply grind the flakes in a coffee grinder for 1 minute. **Serves 4**

CRUNCH TOPPING	KANTEN
¹/₂ cup rolled oats	3 cups unsweetened pear juice
¹/₂ cup pecans, coarsely chopped	¹/₂ teaspoon ground cinnamon
2 tablespoons olive oil	2 tablespoons agar-agar powder
2 tablespoons maple syrup	¹/₄ cup freshly squeezed orange juice
¹/₂ teaspoon vanilla extract	1 teaspoon orange zest
¹/₄ teaspoon ground nutmeg	3 tablespoons maple syrup
Pinch of salt	1 teaspoon vanilla extract
	Pinch of salt

Preheat the oven to 325°F and grease a baking sheet.

Combine all the ingredients for the crunch topping in a bowl and mix well. Spread evenly on the baking sheet and bake for 4 minutes. Toss the ingredients and bake for 4 minutes more, or until the topping is dry. Let cool.

Pour the pear juice into a saucepan. Add the cinnamon. Sprinkle the agar-agar powder over the juice and let soak for 15 minutes. Whisk the juice to remove any agar-agar that has gathered on the bottom of the pot. Bring to a boil, whisking occasionally, then decrease the heat and simmer, uncovered, for 15 minutes, continuing to whisk every few minutes.

Turn off the heat and let cool to room temperature.

Pour the mixture into a blender and add the orange juice, zest, maple syrup, vanilla extract, and salt, and blend for 1 minute. Pour equal amounts of the liquid into 4 wineglasses or martini glasses and chill for 1 hour.

To serve, scatter a generous spoonful of the crunch topping over the kanten.

Agar-Agar: Seaweed for Dessert

Widely available in health food stores, agar-agar, also known as *kanten* or simply *agar*, is a seaweed that acts like gelatin. It is used throughout Southeast Asia to make candies, puddings, and other desserts. In Japan, it has recently been reinvented as a diet food because it contains no fat.

Gelatin, often used in sweets like cheesecake, ice cream, jams, and jellies, is made from cattle bones and hides—by-products of factory farms—that are treated with chemicals before the collagen within is extracted. It's an energy-intensive procedure that conjures some unpleasant images. Making gel from seaweed, however, has a low environmental impact. Cooking with agar-agar takes getting used to, but you'll find that it's adaptable to any flavor and fun to experiment with. Use 30 percent more agar-agar when working with an acidic ingredient like orange juice.

Poached Quince in Orange Blossom Water

Quince smells wonderful, like a pear with notes of citrus. But resist tasting the raw fruit—it is highly tannic until cooked through. Quince require a long cooking time to soften to the point of being edible, and a sharp knife is needed for slicing through their hard flesh, but their delicate flavor is worth the wait and the work. Quince grows in much of the United States— I've even picked some in Central Park—and they are sold at many markets throughout the winter. Serve this dessert on its own or with vanilla ice cream and the easy crunch topping from the Pear Kanten with Pecan Crunch (page 101). **Serves 4**

3/4 cups honey	4 meduim quince, peeled, quartered, and cored
1/3 cup orange blossom water	
Salt	4 teaspoons freshly squeezed lime juice
	12 to 16 fresh mint leaves

Choose a medium-sized saucepan in which to poach the quince, and cut out a circle of parchment paper or wax paper to fit just inside the pan. Set aside the parchment paper.

Bring 4$\frac{1}{2}$ cups water, the honey, orange blossom water, and a dash of salt to a boil in the saucepan, stirring to dissolve the honey. Cut each quince quarter in half to form 2 wedges. Decrease the heat to a simmer. Add the quince to the simmering liquid, and place the parchment directly on top of the quince to cover. The paper should just barely touch the fruit. Simmer, gently stirring once every 30 minutes, until the quince is soft and cooked through, about 1$\frac{1}{2}$ hours. Test a wedge of fruit for doneness; it should be soft and free of its raw tannic taste.

To serve, place the quince in bowls with a few tablespoons of the cooking liquid. Add a teaspoon of lime juice and a few mint leaves to each bowl. Serve hot or cold.

spring

One way to make your meals environmentally friendly is perhaps the most obvious one of all: growing your own organic food! Aside from what it took to get the seeds into your hands, no fossil fuels are needed to get the food onto your table. What's more, gardens or potted plants are perfect places to compost vegetable scraps, and you'll set a good example for your neighbors when they see all of your beautiful produce. Spring is time for tending the garden, and in this chapter I'll provide easy tips for growing food no matter how small your space. I'll also discuss protecting plant diversity and wildlife through the planting of heirloom and native species.

Spring is a season of celebration for the fearless vegetable hunters who prize wild foods, as the earth comes to life with herbs, nuts, and fruits waiting to be plucked. Wild foraging seems exotic to us city dwellers who live far from nature, but it's practiced by people all over the country, including many urbanites. There are delicious edible plants all around us; we need only learn to see them. In this chapter, you'll learn about wild foods like sassafras, nettles, and morel mushrooms, along with simple ways to prepare them.

Growing your own food has many benefits. It allows you to take part in nature's cycles and to gain physical and spiritual satisfaction, a key reason given by so many gardeners for their green addiction. And let's not forget: growing your own food is *cheap*. A source of food that is practically free is nothing to sneeze at in a time when we are likely to see food prices rise, as the true cost of food production catches up with the price tag.

Growing vegetables was once a given part of American life, even in cities. In my neighborhood in Brooklyn, all of the houses were built with backyards that are still planted with vegetables and harvested by my Italian neighbors every summer. From my third-floor perch, I look down at all that space with envy. But with determination and the willingness to climb out of my kitchen window every morning, I've used my fire escape to grow all kinds of herbs, lettuces, tomatoes, and beans, and I've seen friends do the same using rooftop, balcony, and even windowsill space to create lush kitchen gardens.

Even if you only have a fire escape or balcony on which to garden, growing food plants can still be a satisfying experience, especially because a green plant in the middle of a city is a rare treat for the eye. If you have only a sunny windowsill, you can still grow fresh herbs, and because all plants produce oxygen, you'll be helping to purify the air inside your home, too. Many urban dwellers have the option of joining a community garden, where

members are allotted a sizable plot of ground. Look online to find out if there is a garden you can join in your area.

Here are some ideas for growing your own food, while giving a boost to the natural world around you.

HARVESTING THE FRONT YARD

Whatever you decide to plant, the standard place to start is in the backyard. The less obvious choice is to use the front yard, too. In an attempt to reclaim lawns from chemicals, fertilizer, mowers, and water-guzzling sprinklers, many people are choosing to turn their lawn into a space for growing food.

If you have a lot of energy, or want to let friends use a patch of your yard to grow vegetables, you could turn the space into a full-scale garden. If a garden that needs daily attention is too large a commitment, you could plant some fruit and nut trees or berry bushes, turning your lawn into a general snacking area with less of the maintenance work than is required for a full garden. Or, if you simply want to stop using chemicals, gas, and water to maintain your lawn, you could sprinkle native wildflower seeds and let the grass grow out, and surely some edible weeds like clover, chickweed, and dandelion will appear.

Information and classes on gardening are abundant. The best source for gardening guidance might be neighbors, friends, and family with skills to share. If you have a botanic garden in your area, it's a great place to find resources and an active gardening community. Another rich source for knowledge about regional planting is the local Cooperative Extension or Master Gardener program at your state's land-grant university. (See the Gardening websites in the Resources section, page 193.)

BALCONY AND
WINDOWSILL PLANTING

Here are some tricks I've learned from growing plants on my windowsills and fire escape (secretly—don't tell my landlord!) for the last fourteen years.

- Use the ceiling of your balcony and the walls in addition to the floor. Many plants can grow in hanging pots, so if you are handy with a hammer and wires, you can double your growing space.
- Pull flowers off leafy herb plants like parsley, cilantro, basil, and arugula. The flowers make the leaves taste bitter. Try to pluck the flowers before they bloom, or "nip them in the bud," as the flowering communicates to the plant that it has reached the end of its life cycle.
- Use compost for planting and as natural fertilizer and your plants will thrive. Mature compost retains moisture and slowly releases nutrients. If you use homemade compost, keep an eye out, because you never know what dormant seed from meals past will unexpectedly sprout!
- You can plant several different herbs in one pot; just be sure to give them a little space. I usually plant dill, coriander, and mint in the same planter.
- Some plants will survive the winter inside. I bring my rosemary plant inside to a sunny window during the coldest part of winter and water it regularly. Lemon verbena, lemongrass, pineapple sage, and lavender are also known for lasting inside from year to year.
- Keep pets away from plants, as the following can be toxic: chives, scallions, garlic, tomatoes, and potatoes. If you don't want to constantly monitor pets, try building a barrier around the plants using wire netting from a hardware store, or cutting out the top and bottom of a large plastic yogurt container and lodging it in the soil around the plant to form a wall.
- If you buy a seed packet, don't dump all the seeds into the planter (yes, I made this mistake once). Too many plants in one container will compete for water, sunlight, and root space, so sprinkle seeds in moderation, making sure there is space in between.
- AeroGrow, an aeroponic system for growing herbs and plants indoors, can work well when you don't have space with a lot of light. I've never used this, but friends have tried it with success.

107

Plant Heirlooms to Promote Biodiversity

An heirloom seed or plant is one that is genetically unique, selected by farmers over many generations from one harvest to the next based on looks, flavor, and heartiness. Many of these varieties were brought to the United States by immigrant farmers who wanted to bring their region's particular kind of fig, apple, or tomato to grow in the New World.

Growing from heirloom seeds was once standard practice, but over the last sixty years traditional farming has given way to mass-produced hybrid varieties as agriculture has become centralized on large farms, and seeds have been bred to grow anywhere, ripen uniformly, and ship well.

The thousands of unique seed varieties used by small farmers have been reduced in the case of some fruits and vegetables to fewer than ten. This is a significant loss, as heirlooms have developed a natural resistance to regional pests and diseases that mass-produced hybrid seeds have not. Without the genetic diversity of heirlooms, food production is vulnerable to epidemics and infestations.

The Irish potato famine, responsible for the starvation and displacement of millions of people, demonstrates the critical need to keep a wide variety of plant species integrated into our agriculture and diet. In the 1840s, potatoes were the main source of food for Irish peasants. They grew millions of potatoes, but all were of only one variety, called the "lumper." In 1845, a fungus swept through the country that caused the potatoes to rot shortly after being picked. If there had been different types of potatoes growing when the fungus attacked, some would have been immune to the disease, and those with resistant genes could have been planted.

The best way to ensure that heirlooms survive is by planting them in your own little garden. They may have quirky characteristics like bumps and cracks, or keep for a short amount of time after being picked, but the flavor is worth it. Plus, you'll be doing the world a big favor; planting heirloom fruits and vegetables helps the whole species to thrive, not just the one kind you are planting, and it helps to safeguard us against the dangers of a monocrop.

There are thousands of heirloom seeds available, many with poetic names evocative of history and nature: "Cherokee Trail of Tears" pole bean, carried by the Cherokee on their journey of displacement in the 1830s; "Moon and Stars" watermelon, bred by the Amish and named for the bright yellow spots on the leaves and rind of the fruit; and "Washday" peas, known to cook up fast for an easy meal on busy days. There are several places online to find heirloom seeds and resources, including the websites listed in the Resources section (page 193). Or ask your gardener friends and get involved with your local gardening community—you'll find there are countless heirloom enthusiasts eager to share their knowledge and seeds with you!

Sassafras Tea

This refreshing drink needs just a hint of sweetener, as sassafras is naturally quite sweet.
Makes approximately 5 cups

1 small handful sassafras roots, washed in cold water	1 thin slice fresh ginger
¹/₂ cinnamon stick	Maple syrup or honey for serving
	Sparkling water

Using a heavy knife, chop up the sassafras roots or pound them with the handle until you can smell their spicy scent. Place the roots in a saucepan with the cinnamon and 6 cups of water and bring to a boil. Decrease the heat and simmer, partially covered, for 20 minutes. Add the ginger and simmer for 2 minutes more.

Line a fine-mesh strainer with a coffee filter and set over a bowl. Pour the tea through. Sweeten with maple syrup or honey to taste. Drink hot, or serve cold over ice and topped off with sparkling water.

Sassafras: The Original Root Beer

Root beer's flavor originally came from the roots and bark of the sassafras tree, which grows along the Eastern Seaboard. Today, however, most commercial root beer is produced with artificial flavorings, because safrole, a compound in sassafras, was deemed carcinogenic by the FDA. Nevertheless, homemade root beer and sassafras tea are still favorites in many rural kitchens and at state fairs. Above is a recipe for making the tea. Don't worry about overconsumption of safrole, though, because digging up the roots requires too much hard work to drink it in large quantities!

On hikes in spring and summer, look for the distinctive mitten-shaped, three-fingered leaves of foot-high sassafras saplings. Dig down with a pocketknife and pull up the sapling by the root, where there's the most flavor. Don't feel bad about killing a tree; sassafras is often considered invasive because of its rapid proliferation.

Rhubarb Spritzer

Rhubarb (shown opposite), native to Asia, was only introduced to the United States in the 1800s. It now grows throughout the northern part of the country. Every spring rhubarb arrives pretty and pink at the farmers' market, but it's largely passed over because most of us don't know what to do with it except to make pie. This spritzer shows off rhubarb's bright color and tangy taste. Mixed with champagne, it makes a unique and delicate cocktail. **Makes approximately 8 cups**

10 stalks fresh rhubarb	Sparkling water, seltzer, or champagne, for serving
2 cinnamon sticks	4 strawberries, thinly sliced
Honey to taste	1 sprig mint

Slice off the leaves and brown parts from the rhubarb stalks and discard. Rinse the rhubarb stalks and slice into 2-inch pieces. Put the rhubarb slices and cinnamon sticks in a pot and cover with water. Bring to a boil and simmer until the rhubarb is soft, 3 to 4 minutes.

Strain the liquid through a fine-mesh strainer or cheesecloth, pressing as much liquid out of the rhubarb pulp as possible. Whisk in the honey, tasting to adjust the sweetness. Discard the cinnamon and cooked rhubarb (or use the rhubarb to add bulk to a strawberry pie) and let the liquid cool.

To serve, pour into glasses over ice and top off with sparkling water, seltzer, or champagne. Garnish with a few strawberry slices and a mint leaf.

Matzoh Brei with Caramelized Apples

When I was growing up, my mother would make a special treat of fried matzoh, or matzoh brei, during Passover. My sister and I always looked forward to it; it was even better than French toast, its fluffier cousin. Try making this in spring, when matzoh is easy to find in stores. **Serves 4**

2 firm apples, peeled, cored, and quartered

3 tablespoons unsalted butter plus extra, at room temperature

1 teaspoon ground cinnamon

4 tablespoons maple syrup, plus more for serving

3 eggs

1/2 cup milk

1/2 teaspoon vanilla extract

Pinch of salt

6 pieces lightly salted matzoh

Slice each apple quarter lengthwise into 4 pieces. Heat a sauté pan over medium-high heat and add 2 tablespoons of the butter, followed by the apples. Cook the apples, flipping them occasionally, until they are tender and lightly browned, about 6 minutes. Add the cinnamon and 2 tablespoons of the maple syrup and cook for 1 minute. Turn off the heat and transfer the apples to a covered dish to keep warm.

Whisk together the remaining 2 tablespoons maple syrup with the eggs, milk, vanilla extract, and salt. Pour the batter into a pie dish.

Put the matzoh in a large bowl and cover with warm water for 1 minute. Drain the matzoh and gently squeeze to release excess water. Break the matzoh into quarters. If they break unevenly or into small pieces, that's fine. Soak the matzoh in the batter for 2 minutes.

Heat the sauté pan over medium-high heat and add 1 tablespoon of the butter. When the butter is hot, pull several pieces of matzoh out of the batter and put them in the pan. Cook for 1 1/2 minutes. You can drop a teaspoon of batter onto the matzoh here and there as it cooks to make it fluffier, or to join smaller broken pieces together. Flip the matzoh with a spatula and cook on the second side until golden brown, 1 1/2 minutes more. Drop more butter in the pan and repeat with the remaining matzoh and batter.

Serve as soon as it comes out of the pan with the apple slices and extra maple syrup. It will disappear very fast!

The Best Granola Ever

This granola is better than anything I have bought in a store (as homemade foods so often are), if that helps explain its boastful name! I use a mixture of nuts—everything from cashews, pecans, almonds, and peeled hazelnuts to walnuts. Pistachios, however, will burn quickly, so if you're using them, add them at the end and let them bake for just a few minutes. This granola keeps for a long time in the refrigerator, so double the batch if you like. It makes a great gift, too! Serve it with milk or yogurt and fresh fruit. **Makes 8 cups**

2 cups raw nuts, coarsely chopped	6 tablespoons maple syrup
2 cups rolled oats	5 tablespoons olive or canola oil
1 tablespoon ground cinnamon	1 tablespoon vanilla extract
1/2 teaspoon allspice	1 1/2 cups dried apricots, coarsely chopped
1/4 teaspoon ground nutmeg	1/2 cup raw, unsweetened coconut flakes
Salt	3 tablespoons cacao nibs

Preheat the oven to 250°F.

Combine the nuts, oats, cinnamon, allspice, nutmeg, and a dash of salt in a large bowl and stir. Add the maple syrup, 4 tablespoons of the oil, and the vanilla extract and stir.

Spread the granola evenly on a baking sheet and bake for 15 minutes. Stir the granola well, rotate the pan, and bake for 15 minutes more. At this point, the granola should be almost completely dry. Add the apricots and the remaining 1 tablespoon oil to the mixture, stir well, and return the pan to the oven for 5 minutes. Add the coconut flakes and bake for 2 minutes more. Remove the pan from the oven and stir in the cacao nibs.

Let the granola cool before serving.

Stinging Nettle Pesto
with Seared Scallops

Nettles—weeds that grow throughout the United States—are like something out of a scary children's story. Their leaves are serrated like teeth and they're covered with spiky hairs that sting on contact. But the sting is fleeting, and the antidote is the juice of the nettles' own leaves. Boiled briefly, nettles turn into a rich green vegetable much like spinach. Farmed bay scallops are a good seafood choice because they don't require antibiotics or other chemical treatment and they clean the surrounding water by filtering out matter. Serves 4 as a starter

Salt and freshly ground black pepper

$1/4$ pound stinging nettles

$1/4$ cup fresh mint leaves, plus more for garnish

1 clove garlic, minced

$1/2$ cup pine nuts, toasted

$1/4$ cup lemon juice

$1/3$ cup plus 3 tablespoons olive oil

$1/4$ cup firmly packed grated Parmigiano-Reggiano cheese

16 farmed bay scallops

Fill a large pot halfway full with water. Add $1/4$ cup salt and bring to a boil.

Fill the sink or a large bowl with cold water. Using gloves or tongs, submerge the nettles in the water and let them sit for 5 minutes. Remove the nettles and discard the water. Wearing rubber gloves, pull the leaves off of the stems and discard the stems.

Put the nettles in the boiling water and boil for 1 minute. Drain and spread the nettles on a baking sheet. Let cool completely. Squeeze out as much of the water as possible and coarsely chop.

Place the nettles in the bowl of a food processor with the mint, garlic, pine nuts, and 2 tablespoons of the lemon juice. Process until the mixture has formed a paste. With the machine running, pour in $1/3$ cup olive oil. Transfer to a bowl and fold in the cheese. Taste and adjust the seasoning with salt and pepper. Set aside.

Slice off the small side muscle from the scallops, then rinse in cold water and thoroughly pat dry. Season with salt on both sides. Heat a skillet for about 1 minute. Add the 3 tablespoons olive oil and test to make sure it's hot (a drop of liquid should sizzle when it hits the skillet). Place the scallops in the skillet. They should have plenty of room so that they sear instead of steam. If the skillet is small, sear them in batches. Cook the first side for $1^1/2$ minutes, then flip and cook the second side for 1 minute. When done, the scallops should have a brown crust but still be translucent in the center.

Place 4 scallops on a plate and top each with a teaspoon of pesto. Season with the remaining lemon juice, salt, and freshly ground black pepper. Garnish with a few small mint leaves.

Baby Artichokes with Fresh Chervil

Easy to prepare, baby artichokes require only half the work needed for the larger globe variety. Because they're so small, they haven't formed the fuzzy inner choke that requires so much trimming, and they are fully cooked in 20 minutes or less. The herb chervil is in the same family as fennel and has a mild licorice taste. It is slightly sweet and adds a cooling herbal zing to summer dishes. **Serves 4**

12 baby artichokes	Salt and freshly ground black pepper
2 lemons	1 cup vegetable or chicken stock
3 tablespoons olive oil	1/2 bunch fresh chervil, coarsely chopped, plus 4 sprigs fresh chervil for garnish
2 large cloves garlic, minced	

Rinse the artichokes in cold water. Fill a bowl halfway with water and squeeze in the juice of 1 lemon. Slice the second lemon into wedges and set aside.

To trim the artichokes, cut off the stem of each one at the base. Remove the tough green leaves around the base by peeling them back and snapping them off until you reach leaves that are yellow and tender. Slice off the top third of the artichoke and discard. If the artichokes are very small, leave them whole. Otherwise, cut them in half vertically. As you trim each artichoke, drop it into the lemon water to prevent it from turning brown. Repeat until all of the artichokes are trimmed.

Drain the artichokes and heat a large sauté pan over medium-high heat. Add the olive oil and toss in the garlic. Stir for 20 seconds, then add the artichokes and 2 teaspoons salt. Pour in the stock and bring to a boil. Decrease the heat and simmer, covered, until the artichokes are tender, about 20 minutes.

Remove the pan from the heat and stir in the chervil. Taste the broth and season with salt, if needed.

To serve, divide the artichokes among four plates and pour a spoonful of the cooking broth on each. Season with salt and pepper and a wedge of lemon. Garnish each plate with a sprig of chervil.

Eggs and New Potatoes
with Green Olive Pesto

This is a cross between an egg salad and a potato salad, two classic warm-weather dishes that usually rely on mayonnaise for flavor and binding. In this recipe, the creamy texture of the new potatoes pulls the ingredients together, and the nut-and-olive pesto imparts a rich taste. A traditional basil pesto works just as well. Because their skin is thin and delicate, there is no need to peel new potatoes; simply wash them thoroughly. This healthy salad can be eaten in sandwiches or with lightly dressed lettuce greens. **Serves 4 to 6**

5 eggs	6 green olives (preferably the Cerignola variety), pitted
Salt and freshly ground black pepper	$1/4$ cup toasted walnuts
1 tablespoon white or apple cider vinegar	1 tablespoon lemon juice
1 cup finely diced new potatoes or red potatoes (roughly 3 to 4 potatoes)	3 tablespoons olive oil
$1/4$ cup firmly packed fresh flat-leaf parsley leaves	1 celery stalk, halved vertically and thinly sliced
3 anchovy fillets	2 scallions, green and white parts, thinly sliced

Put the eggs in a saucepan with cold water to cover, 1 teaspoon salt, and the vinegar. Bring to a boil, then decrease the heat and simmer, covered, for 1 minute. Turn off the heat and let the eggs sit in the water, covered, for 15 minutes. Drain the eggs and transfer to a bowl of ice water. When cool, peel and finely chop the eggs and put them in a large bowl.

Put the potatoes in a saucepan with cold water to cover and a dash of salt. Bring to a boil, then decrease the heat and simmer, covered, until just tender, about 4 minutes. Drain and let the potatoes cool. Add the potatoes to the eggs.

Combine the parsley, anchovies, olives, walnuts, and lemon juice in the bowl of a food processor and pulse until coarsely ground. With the food processor running, slowly pour in the olive oil. The pesto should have a coarse texture, so turn off the machine once all of the oil has been poured in to prevent overprocessing.

Gently toss the pesto with the eggs and potatoes. Fold in the celery and scallions. Season with salt and plenty of pepper.

Grow Native Plants to Support Wildlife

The best way to attract friendly native insects and birds is to let native plants—the ones that have been around for at least a couple of centuries—flourish in your garden. In addition to providing natural security against pests, turning your garden into a haven for plant-friendly wildlife gives them a much-needed helping hand as their wild habitat disappears.

Native flora supports native fauna because the plants and animals evolved side by side. Most animals, including the creatures at the bottom of the food chain that we generally fail to notice, can't nourish themselves on foreign plants. But even these lowly beings have a huge impact on our ecosystem, because if they disappear, so do all the animals above them on the food chain—the charismatic wild animals that we pay homage to in pictures and poetry, like wolves, owls, and turtles. We can help these animals to thrive by planting native species.

The process of pollination is one of nature's foundations. It happens when pollen is moved within flowers, or from one flower to another within the same species, ensuring that a plant will produce healthy fruit and be capable of germinating. Pollen can be moved by the wind, but most of the time it is moved by animals, including bees, wasps, birds, bats, butterflies, moths, and beetles. We want to attract pollinators to our gardens to not only help our food grow, but also to provide nourishment and shelter for these creatures whose habitat has diminished through pesticide use, pollution, and the clearing of wild land. If we don't help to protect these pollinators, many of which are endangered, the effects on the natural world could be extreme.

To draw beneficial insects into your garden, plant flowers and other plants that they like. Some insects are very small—like tiny pollinating wasps that don't sting humans—so they favor tiny blossoms like the ones that grow on mint and other herbs. But once herbs begin to flower, the leaves become bitter. If you are growing parsley, basil, arugula, and other herbs in your kitchen garden, you should pick off the flowers and add them to your salad as soon as they appear. If you are also trying to provide food for pollinators, a good solution is to plant more than one basil plant, for example, and leave the flowers on the ones you care to donate to the birds and bees. Once a week, pick off the flowers—it will make the plant thicker and stronger, and the flowers will reappear in a few days. The good insects you attract will devour garden pests and then harvest the nectar and pollen from the flowers.

Following is a list of food-bearing or edible flora whose blossoms attract pollinators. This is only a partial list, however, as there are many plants the world over that attract pollinators, and sometimes bees are just plain fickle and will surprise you in what they're in the mood for! You can grow most of these on a sunny balcony, and many of them on a windowsill. For a few, you will likely need a yard.

HERBS

- Bee balm or bergamot
- Borage
- Cilantro
- Dill
- Fennel
- Lemon balm
- Lemongrass
- Oregano
- Parsley
- Rosemary
- Sage
- Thyme

VEGETABLES

- Buckwheat (technically, a grass)
- Cucumber
- Flowering broccoli
- Melon (Haogen and Eden's Gem varieties)
- Radish
- Squash (most varieties)
- Tomato (all heirloom varieties)

TREES AND SHRUBS

- Blueberry
- Elderberry
- Maple
- Sassafras

Much of this information was culled from the Pollinator Partnership website (see the Resources section, page 193, for their website). When you type in your zip code, the site will tell you your "eco-region" and list all the native plants in that region that attract pollinators, along with the specific pollinators drawn to that plant.

The following simple tools can also be very effective in attracting friendly wild-life to your garden:

- **Water:** Provides a place for dragonflies to breed and for birds to drink. A small container will do.
- **Logs and rocks:** A pile of rocks or a few decomposing logs off to the side of your garden will attract frogs and toads, who in turn eat slugs and snails, some of the gardener's worst enemies.
- **Bird feeder:** Provides a place for birds to find food in the winter.

119

Watercress with
Roasted Enoki Mushrooms and Peas

Enoki mushrooms are also known as "snowpuffs" or "golden needle" mushrooms because of their long, stretched stems and white caps. They come to us from Japan, where they are served raw or lightly cooked. Enoki are usually sold refrigerated in sealed plastic packets of 3.5 to 7 ounces. Despite their delicate appearance, they have a surprisingly meaty texture, especially when roasted. Mirin, or rice wine, is a sweet Japanese cooking wine that has a low alcohol content. If you can't find mirin, substitute a tablespoon of honey mixed with a drop of white wine. **Serves 2 to 4**

Salt and freshly ground black pepper

2 cups shelled green peas

1 tablespoon soy sauce

1 tablespoon mirin

2 tablespoons sweet white miso

1/4 cup olive oil

7 ounces fresh enoki mushrooms, roots trimmed off at the base of the cluster

3 tablespoons rice vinegar

1 bunch watercress, coarsely chopped

2 scallions, green and white parts, julienned and cut into 1-inch lengths

Preheat the oven to 425°F. Line a baking sheet with parchment paper.

Bring a small saucepan of salted water to a boil and add the peas. As soon as the water returns to a boil, drain the peas and blanch in cold water. Set aside.

In a large bowl, whisk together the soy sauce, mirin, miso, and olive oil. Spread the enokis on the baking sheet, then the peas, and spoon 3 tablespoons of the marinade over the top. Roast the vegetables for 6 minutes. Remove from the oven and let cool.

Whisk the vinegar into the remaining soy sauce marinade to make a dressing. Add the watercress and scallions and toss. Add the enokis and peas and gently fold them into the bowl. Season with several grinds of pepper. Serve immediately.

Fava Beans and Seared Zucchini with Garlicky Croutons

This dish pops with the bright flavor of fresh ingredients cooked quickly; but while the final "zap" is quick, preparation of this aromatic salad takes time. Enjoy it: you'll use several cooking techniques, from searing zucchini to making croutons to preparing favas. For a shortcut, use store-bought croutons or buy shelled favas. Favas need to be peeled twice: First, pull the beans out of the pod by pulling on the stem and unzipping the side; then, after cooking, peel the thin layer of skin from each bean. Serves 4

2 cups shelled (or 1¹/₂ pounds in the pod) fresh fava beans

Salt and freshly ground black pepper

5 tablespoons olive oil, plus extra

1¹/₂ cloves garlic, minced

1 tablespoon dried thyme

A few slices of stale baguette or other crusty bread, crust removed and coarsely diced

2 zucchini

¹/₂ cup firmly packed fresh mint leaves

¹/₂ cup loosely packed Parmesan or other hard Italian cheese, shaved

2 tablespoons lemon juice

Preheat the oven to 375°F.

Put the favas in a small pot with water to cover. Add 1 tablespoon of salt and bring to a boil, then reduce the heat and simmer, uncovered, until the favas are just tender, about 4 minutes. Drain and cool in an ice bath. Peel off the skin and set the beans aside.

To make the croutons, in a large bowl whisk together 2 tablespoons of the olive oil with 1 clove of the minced garlic, the thyme, and 1 teaspoon salt. Add the bread and toss to coat evenly. Spread the bread on a baking sheet. Bake for 5 minutes, stir, then continue baking until the croutons are crisp and golden, about 5 minutes more. Taste and season with salt. Let cool, then set the croutons aside in an airtight container.

Trim the ends of the zucchini and cut them in half. Cut the halves into slices ¹/₄ inch thick and season with salt. Heat a skillet and add 2 tablespoons of the olive oil. Working in batches, lay several slices of the zucchini on the skillet. Turn after 2 minutes and cook on the second side for 1 minute, until the zucchini is cooked through but still firm. While searing, drizzle the zucchini with more oil as needed. Transfer to a plate and repeat with the remaining zucchini. Allow to cool to room temperature.

Cut the zucchini into large bite-sized pieces and toss with the remaining ¹/₂ clove of minced garlic, the favas, mint, Parmesan, lemon juice, and the remaining 1 tablespoon olive oil. Season with salt and pepper.

Plate the salad and top with the croutons. Serve immediately.

Fava Plants and Reducing Pesticide Use

The appearance of fava beans always causes a stir at the farmers' market because their return signals the beginning of warm-weather produce. Besides being tasty, favas are an important crop for maintaining healthy soil. Their deep taproots help to loosen compacted soil, and fava plants also produce large amounts of nitrogen, much of which goes back into the soil and sustains subsequent crops. More nitrogen in the soil means less chemical fertilizer sprayed on plants. Scientists are experimenting with growing favas next to other vegetables so that the nitrogen is transferred directly from the roots of the favas to the roots of the other plants.

Lamb's Quarters and Pea Shoots Soup

This lighter take on cold spinach soup gets its rich texture from potatoes instead of the traditional cream. Lamb's quarters grow wild and are sometimes considered a weed, but they taste like chard or spinach when cooked. Pea shoots are the young leaves and tendrils of pea plants (shown below). Long used in Chinese cooking, pea shoots have a strong, fresh pea flavor. **Serves 4**

3 tablespoons olive oil

2 stalks green garlic, or 4 scallions, coarsely chopped

2 Yukon Gold potatoes, peeled and sliced ¼ inch thick

Salt and freshly ground black pepper

4 cups vegetable or chicken stock

2 large handfuls lamb's quarters, coarsely chopped

2 large handfuls pea shoots, coarsely chopped

Juice of 1 lemon

4 teaspoons chopped fresh chives for garnish

Heat a stockpot over medium-high heat, add the oil, and then add the green garlic. Cook, stirring frequently, until soft, about 5 minutes. Add the potatoes and 2 teaspoons salt, stir, and pour in the stock. Cover the pot and bring to a boil. Decrease the heat and simmer, covered, until the potatoes are soft, about 10 minutes.

Stir in the lamb's quarters, cover, and cook until the leaves are soft but still bright green, about 4 minutes. Add the pea shoots and cook for another minute. Pour the soup into a blender and blend until smooth. Add salt and pepper to taste.

Serve warm or cold, garnished with a dash of lemon juice and a teaspoon of chives.

Ash-e-reshteh (Persian New Year's Soup with Beans, Noodles, and Herbs)

This countrified soup is often served in late March for Norooz, the Persian new year. With beans, vegetables, noodles, and yogurt, it is a meal in itself. If you can't find fava beans, use limas. Start this recipe the night before to soak the chickpeas, kidneys beans, and fava beans. Boil them in a pot with four cups of water for one minute, then turn off the heat and add a splash of apple cider vinegar. Cover the pot and let them soak overnight. **Serves 6 to 8**

¹/₂ cup chickpeas, soaked overnight in water to cover

¹/₄ cup kidney beans, soaked overnight in water to cover

¹/₂ cup dried fava beans, soaked overnight in water to cover, or 1¹/₂ cups frozen lima beans

3 yellow onions

7 tablespoons olive oil

5 cloves garlic, minced

1 teaspoon ground turmeric

¹/₄ cup dried lentils

14 cups vegetable or chicken stock

Salt

1 large handful fresh mint leaves, torn into pieces

6 ounces thin egg noodles or linguine, broken into thirds

1 bunch leafy greens, stemmed, and coarsely chopped

¹/₄ cup fresh dill leaves, minced

¹/₂ cup fresh cilantro, minced

¹/₂ cup fresh flat-leaf parsley, minced

2 cups plain yogurt

Dice 1 of the onions. Heat a large pot over medium-high heat and add 4 tablespoons of the olive oil. Add the onion and sauté until lightly browned, about 5 minutes. Drain and rinse the chickpeas, kidney beans, and fava beans, and add them to the onion along with 4 of the minced cloves of garlic, the turmeric, and lentils. Sauté for 1 minute, then add the stock and bring to a boil. Boil the beans, covered, for 1 hour. Tilt the lid so the pot is partially covered and simmer, stirring occasionally, for 1¹/₂ hours. Season with salt.

Slice the remaining 2 onions into thin half moons. Heat a sauté pan over high heat and add the remaining 3 tablespoons olive oil. Add the onions and fry, stirring frequently, until the onions are brown and caramelized. Add the remaining garlic and the mint and sauté for 1 minute. Season with salt and set aside.

Add the noodles to the soup and cook until tender, 6 to 8 minutes. When the noodles are almost done, add the leafy greens and the fresh herbs and cook for 2 minutes.

Serve with a large dollop of yogurt and a few tablespoons of the sautéed onion mixture.

Almost any food in the world is available to us today, but as we wean ourselves from an economy based on cheap fossil fuels, the price of exotic fare will increase, and locally foraged foods may play a bigger role in our diets. Before the development of agriculture, we were all hunter-gatherers, and, happily, the natural world is still brimming with sustenance.

Contrary to what you might think, you don't have to go to the woods to find wild edibles. In the last few years I've spent time exploring the rural *and* urban outdoors with knowledgeable foragers, often in New York City, where a favorite haunt of foragers is Manhattan's Central Park! If we can find food in the middle of this nation's most densely populated city, then imagine how much more the rest of the country has to offer. Some of the wild foraged foods I've found, in Manhattan as well as other parts of the country, include:

- Apples
- Bay leaves
- Black walnuts
- Blackberries
- Blueberries
- Calendula
- Chanterelle mushrooms
- Chickweed
- Chives
- Daylilies
- Elderberries
- Epazote
- Garlic mustard
- Ginkgo nuts
- Hawthorn berries
- June berries
- Lamb's quarters
- Mint
- Mulberries
- Nettles
- Persimmons
- Quince
- Ramps (wild leeks)
- Raspberries
- Sassafras
- Shiso
- Sumac

Foraging reminds us of the vitality of our environment. Not only do animals live in green spaces, but so do countless flowers, plants, and trees that are reliable sources of food. And it's easy to forget, but most medicines were originally derived from plants.

In some situations, it's easy to identify what's edible, like when walking in Maine surrounded by wild blueberries. Hunting wild mushrooms and deciding which ones are safe to eat, however, is a skill that can take years to learn. On your own, it can be intimidating, but fortunately there are so many "mycofreaks" (mushroom enthusiasts) around that help is never far away. Do some investigating in your area and you, too, might be able to join a mushroom-hunting trip such as the one I recently saw advertised in Maryland, where for $100 you can be blindfolded and driven to a mushroom enclave by the likes of "Deaner" and "Freightrain" to gather as much as you can carry. (Don't share the secret location, though; that's a serious violation of the mushroom hunter's code of honor!)

Mushrooms really deserve their own subgenre of foraging. All across America, Europe, and Asia, mushroom hunting is a favorite pastime, and wild mushrooms garner a high price per pound because of their rich taste and powerful medicinal properties. In the United States, mushroom hunting inspires an obsession similar to what some people feel toward sports. There are wild mushroom festivals, clothing companies, and art galleries, and even wild mushroom social clubs.

It's easy to go online and find mushroom hunting and other foraging resources in your area. In many cities, "wild stalking" classes with experienced foragers are easy to find. Throughout the year there are guided foraging walks through Central Park in Manhattan. Any region where wild mushrooms grow has its own local mycological (the study of mushrooms) society, sponsoring lectures and foraging walks. And many guidebooks are available to help you identify wild foods (see the Resources section on page 194 for a list of wild foraging books). So go grab a book or take a class and tap into the bounty that is all around us!

Orecchiette with Morel Mushrooms and Garlic Ramps

This recipe pairs two foods you might find on a spring hike: morels and ramps, the latter being the wild leeks that grow from South Carolina to Canada. Both have the fresh earthiness of spring, tempered here by the richness of Grana Padano and mascarpone. Buying morels can get expensive, so if you can only afford a few, you can make up for it by adding another portobello or two. If you can't find the pasta called orecchiette (literally, "little ears"), use small shells or another bite-size pasta. **Serves 4**

20 garlic ramps	$1/2$ cup dry white wine
4 tablespoons olive oil	Zest of 1 lemon
Salt and freshly ground black pepper	$1/2$ teaspoon ground nutmeg
2 cups dried orecchiette	$1/4$ cup grated Grana Padano or Pecorino Romano cheese
4 portobello mushrooms, diced	
2 cloves garlic, minced	Minced fresh flat-leaf parsley leaves for garnish
15 morel mushrooms, quartered lengthwise	4 tablespoons mascarpone

Trim the roots from the ramps with a paring knife, and remove any dead skin clinging to the bulbs. Wash the ramps a few times in warm water to remove the dirt. Coarsely chop the leaves and set them aside. Slice the bulbs down the middle and set aside.

Add 2 tablespoons of the olive oil to a large pot of salted water and bring to a boil. When the water is boiling, stir in the orecchiette and cook until al dente, about 10 minutes.

Heat a large sauté pan over medium-high heat and add the remaining 2 tablespoons olive oil. Add the ramp bulbs and sauté for 2 minutes. Add the portobellos and cook until soft, about 4 minutes, stirring often. Add the garlic and morels and cook for 2 minutes more. Pour in the wine and simmer gently, uncovered, for 10 minutes.

When the pasta is ready, drain, reserving $1/4$ cup of the cooking water. Add the pasta and the cooking water to the mushrooms along with the ramp leaves, lemon zest, and nutmeg, and cook on high for 2 minutes.

Serve the pasta piping hot with grated Grana Padano over the top. Garnish with the minced parsley and season with freshly ground black pepper. Finish each serving with 1 tablespoon of mascarpone spooned on top.

Almond Tofu with Snap Peas and Soba Noodles

With baking, the texture of tofu turns satisfyingly dense and chewy. In many cities, you can find fresh and creamy locally-made tofu at farmers' markets, food co-ops, and in Asian markets. Tender spring snap peas are quick to cook; here they are simply placed in a colander and cooked with the hot water from the soba noodles. **Serves 4**

14 ounces extra-firm tofu, drained and sliced crosswise ¹/₄ inch thick

Salt

6 tablespoons almond butter

2 tablespoons soy sauce

3 tablespoons maple syrup

1 tablespoon sesame oil

3 scallions, green and white parts, thinly sliced

5 tablespoons olive oil, plus more for the baking sheet

1 tablespoon minced fresh ginger

2 cloves garlic, minced

3 cups snap peas, trimmed and halved diagonally

8 ounces soba noodles

2 tablespoons rice vinegar

Leaves from 1 bunch fresh cilantro

Chili oil

Preheat the oven to 350°F.

Lay the tofu slices on a well-oiled baking sheet and season with salt.

In a small bowl, whisk together the almond butter, soy sauce, maple syrup, and sesame oil. Rub ¹/₂ teaspoon of the almond butter mixture into the top of each tofu slice. Try not to get the sauce on the pan. Bake for 25 minutes. Flip the tofu and season lightly with salt. Rub the second side of each tofu slice with ¹/₂ teaspoon of the almond butter mixture, reserving the extra. Bake for 25 minutes more. Let cool.

Slice the tofu lengthwise into strips. Heat a sauté pan over high heat and add 2 tablespoons of the olive oil. Add the scallions, cook for 1 minute, and add the tofu and ginger. Cook the tofu for 1 minute, undisturbed. Add the garlic and ¹/₄ cup water and sauté over medium-high heat for 2 minutes. Turn off the heat and stir in the reserved almond butter mixture. Leave the pan on the stove, covered.

Put the peas in a colander in the sink. Bring a large pot of salted water to a boil. Add the noodles and return to a boil, then simmer, uncovered, for 6 minutes, until the noodles are just cooked through. Pour the noodles on top of the peas in the colander and drain out the water. Immediately pour the noodles and peas back into the pot. Add the remaining 3 tablespoons olive oil and toss to prevent the noodles from sticking. Stir in the tofu, rice vinegar, cilantro, and salt to taste.

Serve immediately with the chili oil alongside.

Miso-Glazed Striped Bass
with Shiso Cucumber Salad

Shiso, also known as "beefsteak plant," is a pungent, wild-tasting herb native to North America but typically sold only in Japanese markets. Often served with sushi, shiso is essential here for bringing the flavor of the fish to life. Dry sake served cold rounds out this dish well.
Serves 4

MARINADE

2 tablespoons freshly grated ginger

4 cloves garlic

1/4 cup sweet white miso

1/4 cup mirin

2 tablespoons sesame oil

2 tablespoons soy sauce

1/4 cup Dijon mustard

3 tablespoons olive oil

2 pounds U.S.-farmed striped bass, rinsed and patted dry

2 medium or 4 small turnips, diced

4 tablespoons plus 1 dash olive oil

6 shiso leaves

6 red radishes

1 large cucumber, halved, seeded, and sliced 1/4 inch thick

2 large handfuls mild lettuce

2 tablespoons rice vinegar

Salt

Black sesame seeds (optional)

Preheat the oven to 400°F.

Blend all the marinade ingredients together in a blender. Place the fish in a casserole dish. Set aside 3 tablespoons of the marinade. Cover the fish with the rest of the marinade and let sit in the refrigerator for 30 minutes.

Put the turnips in a shallow baking dish and toss with the reserved marinade and a dash of olive oil. Cover and bake until they are tender, about 30 minutes. Remove the turnips from the oven but keep them covered.

Julienne the shiso leaves and radishes and combine them in a large bowl. Add the cucumbers, but do not toss them together. Set the bowl aside in the refrigerator.

Heat an ovenproof skillet over medium heat. Add 2 tablespoons of the olive oil and sear the fish skin side up, until well browned, about 4 minutes. Baste the fish with the reserved marinade, then flip the fish and sear for 4 minutes on the second side. The fish is done when it is opaque inside.

Add the lettuce, the remaining 2 tablespoons olive oil, the rice vinegar, and a dash of salt to the salad and toss.

To serve, put a scoop of turnips on each plate with a piece of fish and the salad. Pour the cooking sauce over the fish and garnish with the sesame seeds, if desired.

Spot Prawns with Garlic, Sorrel, and White Wine

Lemony sorrel brightens the flavor of spot prawns, large shrimp that can be served with the head and tail on or peeled. To remove the shell, use scissors to cut down the back to the tail tip. Like all shrimp, prawns only take a minute or two to cook, and after that can become tough. Millet provides a fluffy bed that soaks up the sauce. Start this recipe the night before serving so that the millet can soak. Serves 4

1 cup millet, soaked in cold water for 1 to 12 hours and drained	1 bunch sorrel, trimmed
1/2 cup almonds, coarsely chopped	1/4 cup white wine
7 tablespoons olive oil	1/4 cup vegetable or chicken stock
Salt and freshly ground black pepper	11/4 pounds spot prawns, peeled, deveined, and thawed
2 shallots, thinly sliced	2 cloves garlic, minced
1 bunch green Swiss chard, stems removed and coarsely chopped	1/2 teaspoon red pepper flakes
	1 tablespoon unsalted butter

In a saucepan or teakettle, bring 2 cups water to a boil. In a separate saucepan, heat the millet over medium heat, stirring frequently, until it is mostly dry. Stir in the almonds, 3 tablespoons of the olive oil, and 1 1/2 teaspoons salt. Add the boiling water to the millet. Decrease the heat and simmer, covered, for 30 minutes. Turn off the heat and let the millet rest, covered, for 5 minutes. Fluff with a fork and set aside.

Heat a skillet over medium-high heat and add 2 tablespoons of the olive oil. Add the shallots and cook until they begin to brown, then add the chard and sorrel and cook until slightly wilted, about 1 minute. Add the wine and stock, and bring to a boil. Decrease the heat slightly and simmer, uncovered, for 5 minutes, to let the liquid reduce and thicken. Season to taste with salt.

Transfer the greens and cooking liquid to a large bowl. Heat the skillet over high heat and add the remaining 2 tablespoons olive oil. Add the prawns and cook for 1 minute, undisturbed, until the bottoms turn pink. Season the prawns with salt. Add the garlic and red pepper flakes and cook for 1 minute, stirring constantly. Add the greens to the prawns and cook everything together for 30 seconds. Turn off the heat and stir in the butter. Taste and season.

To serve, put a few heaping spoonfuls of millet on each plate, followed by the prawns. Pour the sauce over the top and season with pepper.

Wild-caught spot prawns from British Columbia are a responsible seafood choice because they are caught with underwater traps, which, although they attract fish, hold them alive until they can be released. The problem with many other types of shrimp is that they are usually caught using trawl nets that catch every-thing in their path, including endangered species. A typical shrimp fishery hauls in 3 to 15 pounds of unwanted animals that are returned to the sea dead for every pound of shrimp caught, so the method used for catching spot prawns is far more eco-friendly.

Carob Pudding

I usually advise people not to compare carob to chocolate because the two tastes are quite distinct. But in this rich pudding, you may find that you like carob even better than chocolate. Originally from the Mediterranean, carob was brought to the United States by Spanish missionaries. It grows in the drier parts of the west, including Arizona and California, so it doesn't have to make the same long, fuel-guzzling trip to us that its tropical nemesis chocolate does. **Serves 4**

2 ripe avocados	2 teaspoons vanilla extract
6 tablespoons unsweetened carob powder	$1/4$ teaspoon salt
$1/2$ cup plus 2 tablespoons maple syrup	$1/8$ teaspoon ground nutmeg
3 tablespoons freshly squeezed lemon juice	1 ripe banana (optional)
	$1/4$ cup chopped nuts (optional)

Place all of the ingredients except the banana and nuts in the bowl of a food processor and process until smooth. Chill for 1 hour before serving.

To serve, spoon some of the pudding into a bowl or glass. Thinly slice the banana (if using) and place several slices on top. Top with chopped nuts if desired.

Rhubarb and Pistachios
over Thick Yogurt

This strikingly colorful dessert pairs tart rhubarb with rich Greek-style yogurt. Use a light-colored honey that won't dull the rhubarb's bright hue. If you are using regular yogurt, start this recipe the night before so that it can strain overnight. **Serves 4**

4 stalks rhubarb, ends and leaves trimmed	1 teaspoon vanilla extract
1/2 teaspoon cardamom	1 teaspoon rose water
1/4 teaspoon ground nutmeg	2 cups Greek-style yogurt, or 4 cups regular yogurt, drained overnight (see page 192) and refrigerated
Pinch of salt	
1/2 cup light-colored honey	1/2 cup pistachios, coarsely chopped

Cut the rhubarb into 1-inch pieces and put in a small saucepan with 1/4 cup water. Cover and bring to a boil, then decrease the heat and simmer, stirring occasionally. When the rhubarb starts to soften, after about 5 minutes, stir in the cardamom, nutmeg, and salt. Break up any large pieces of rhubarb with a wooden spoon. Continue to simmer, covered, until the rhubarb is completely softened, about 4 minutes more. Remove from the heat and stir in the honey and vanilla extract. Let cool. Add the rose water.

To serve, put 1/2 cup of yogurt in each bowl and top with a few tablespoons of the rhubarb. Scatter a few tablespoons of pistachios over the top.

summer

June, July, and August offer such a wide range of fresh foods that it's hard to know what to choose. It's tempting to get stuck in a joyful rut eating beloved classics like corn, tomatoes, and blueberries, but venturing away from the familiar can reward you with new favorites. In this chapter, you'll discover recipes that use poblano chiles, puntarelles, and apricots, and explore new ways of preparing wonderful old standbys—many in dishes that require little to no heat for low-maintenance meals that keep you cool in the kitchen.

Summer heat calls for amped up hydration, and the first drink we reach for is water, often from a plastic bottle. While it can sometimes taste better than tap water, bottled water can have damaging environmental consequences. We'll look at why tap water may be the better, even healthier, choice in the long run. A highlight of summer's bounty is fresh fish and seafood, but in recent years questions about the purity of seafood and the danger of our favorite fish choices becoming extinct have dampened many people's enjoyment. In this chapter, you'll learn how to select fish and seafood with a clear conscience and support healthy fish populations with your dollars. You'll also find fresh ideas for preparing fish here and throughout the book.

I feel lucky to live in New York City, because our drinking water has the reputation of being some of the best in the world. I hope it's as clean as they say, because I've been drinking a lot of it for a long time, but the choice has been easy: I can either drink tap water that is virtually free, or pay more than $1,000 a year for bottled water.

The problem with bottled water is not just its retail price. Plastic bottles are derived from petroleum, and transported through the use of oil. Roughly 2 billion bottles are shipped to the United States yearly, creating thousands of tons of air pollution. Only about 13 percent of plastic bottles get recycled, while most pile up in landfills.

Still, one must balance those facts against the recent finding that, along with chemicals and bacteria, significant trace amounts of prescription drugs have been detected in tap water throughout the country.

As eco-conscious citizens trying to lead healthy lives, we are put in a tough position. What is the right choice—tap water or bottled? The bigger issue may be the value of our public drinking water. A clean water system is part of what should be expected from a responsible government. But the more we choose bottled water over tap, the less government support there will be for maintaining a safe public water supply, the loss of which is almost beyond imagining. It's easy to take

it for granted, but in most of the world, even in some of the wealthiest countries, people cannot turn on a tap and access potable water. Our public water supply is a national treasure that deserves to be maintained at all costs.

The more we protect our public water, by urging legislators to enforce and strengthen the Clean Water Act, the less there is a need for bottled water. For example, the New York–based clean water watchdog group Riverkeeper is pushing the city to restore public water fountains. This simple act would reduce the need to consume bottled water, thus reducing litter, lightening dependence on foreign oil, and shrinking the city's carbon footprint. With growing pollution and population levels, and urban sprawl encroaching on water tables, speaking out and taking action is essential to preserving a healthy public water supply.

ALTERNATIVES TO BOTTLED WATER

You might find that drinking tap water is quite an appealing choice once you know all your options—and there are quite a few. Here I've outlined several methods of breaking the plastic bottle habit that range in price and level of effort required to implement them.

Straight from the Tap

If you are fortunate enough to live in an area where the tap water quality is high, like San Francisco or New York City, use tap water with as little fuss as possible. To improve the taste, add a dash of lemon juice, a slice of orange, or a fresh berry. Chilling water can also do the trick.

Boiled

Boil tap water for a few minutes, let it cool, then shake it up in a sealed container. The movement helps to incorporate air back into the water, as it can taste flat after boiling. I've found that this process makes the water taste mild and pure. This method can be time consuming, but you could turn boiling the water into a nightly ritual, letting it cool overnight.

Filtered

There are many ways to filter water, including point-of-entry filters, which treat water before it gets distributed throughout a home, and point-of-use filters, like the ones that fit in a countertop pitcher, on a spigot, or under a sink. The array of choices is surprising, and the more advanced the system the higher the price tag. The Natural Resources Defense Council (NRDC) website contains a detailed description of different filter types and which substances they remove from the water. See the NRDC website, www.nrdc.org/water/drinking/gfilters .asp, for the "Consumer Guide to Water Filters."

Because of the efforts of a citizen group called Take Back The Filter, the water filter manufacturer Brita now recycles the plastic filters used in its pitch-

ers, so you don't have to feel bad about throwing them in the trash after they've expired. If you want to save money and you're not afraid of an electric drill, you can reuse those same plastic filters with a relatively easy DIY solution: hack into your countertop water purifier. I found clear, simple directions for this process online at www.instructables.com/id/How-to-refill-a-disposable-Brita-brand-water-pit/.

Bubbly

Seltzer used to be a staple in many homes. It was delivered to the door in reusable glass bottles, like milk, and empties were picked up and used again. A few companies have revived this system and are delivering door-to-door in New York and San Francisco. If you're a seltzer devotee, that's one way to get around the plastic bottles in which fizzy water is usually sold.

Another option is to make seltzer yourself, using water from the tap. Several online stores sell siphon bottles that fit a single-use carbonation cartridge that charges the water with carbon dioxide.

A home soda fountain can be installed by a plumber under a kitchen sink or in a cabinet. These can make up to 30 gallons of seltzer before the cartridge needs changing, but the high price makes them better suited to a business than a home. To see all of the different seltzer options online, simply do a search for "seltzer makers" and "seltzer delivery" in your area.

Fish for Dinner?
We're Going to Need a Smaller Boat

The world loves to eat fish. For health reasons, and in order to feed growing populations, Europe, Asia, and the United States are consuming fish at record levels. Sadly, regulations on fishing and fish farming are lax in most countries. The fishing industry wants to cash in on our taste for fish; unfortunately, pollution, overfishing, and harm to endangered species are the unintended consequences of the race to bring ever more product to market. A 2006 study by an international group of scientists found that all saltwater fish and seafood populations will disappear by 2048 if current fishing practices continue. A food source that humans have depended upon for thousands of years may be gone within a few generations. But the loss wouldn't simply affect our food supply; sea creatures filter toxins from the ocean, protect shorelines, and help control destructive algae blooms.

Fortunately, there are solutions on the table, and some have been put into practice with great success.

ECO-FRIENDLY FISHING PRACTICES

Below are some of the effective and imaginative approaches to help us harvest fish with an eye toward the long term. The question now is how to implement these tactics worldwide before all of our wild fish populations are destroyed.

Curbing Bycatch

Bycatch are the unwanted fish and sealife, including birds and sea turtles, that are trapped and killed in industrial fishing nets by the thousands. In recent years, improved fishing gear has begun to reduce the problem by letting nontarget animals escape. There are trap doors for turtles, and electronic beepers or "pingers" that warn mammals like whales to stay away from nets. Catching the shrimp in traps instead of nets lets fishermen release 98 percent of unwanted catch, which is why you'll find "trap-caught" shrimp given a high eco-friendly seafood rating.

Marine Parks

These are the underwater equivalent of national parks, providing a sanctuary where fish are insulated from harmful fishing practices, pollution, and deadly underwater noise from sonar, air guns, and shipping. According to the NRDC, marine parks situated off the coasts of California and Hawaii have an average of twice as many fish as unprotected areas.

Catch Shares

In this arrangement, now successfully being used in Alaska, on the West Coast, and in New England, fisheries are guaranteed a percentage of the overall catch and are rewarded financially for leaving breeding fish to spawn the following season. This helps to preserve healthy oceans, the source of their income. This approach is fundamentally different from the traditional quota system known as "race-to-fish," where fisheries have a limited number of days to catch as much fish as possible.

CHOOSE FISH RESPONSIBLY

We can steer the fishing industry toward responsible practices by buying seafood caught and raised according to these guidelines. When you eat fish, choose those that are farmed or caught sustainably. There are many online lists of the best and worst fish to eat from an ecological perspective. Two sources I consult are the Environmental Defense Fund's Seafood Selector and the Monterey Bay Aquarium's Seafood Watch Guide (find their websites in the Resources section, on page 194). Both provide lists that grade fish on how responsibly they are caught or farmed. They have information on where and how each type of fish is brought to market, as well as recipes to help with preparing unfamiliar types.

Some of my favorite choices from the recommended seafood list include white anchovies, sablefish (also known as black cod or butterfish) caught in Alaska or British Columbia, and wreckfish, a tasty basslike fish caught in the Atlantic Ocean.

Try cooking with new kinds of fish that have a high eco-friendly rating, or if you're at a restaurant and see a fish on the menu that you don't recognize, ask the waiter for a description and try ordering it. The idea is to get away from repeatedly choosing overfished and irresponsibly farmed species, like tuna and salmon. There is usually a sustainable alternative to your favorite endangered fish, with a similar texture and flavor. For example, try Pacific halibut instead of white hake; pole-caught mahimahi from the United States in place of snapper; or U.S.-caught stone crab or Dungeness crab in place of skate.

In addition, you can help to change the marketplace by speaking up at your fish purveyor and at restaurants. Ask where your fish came from, how it was caught, or if it was raised. Go to restaurants with your list of eco-friendly fish in hand and refer to it when you read the menu. Restaurants and purveyors should be able to tell you where their fish is from so you can make thoughtful purchases.

There is always the route of political action. You might get involved with letter-writing campaigns to support issues you care about, such as legislation to protect whales from deadly navy sonar, restrictions on bottom trawling near coral, or creating marine reserves. Your voice can make a big difference. Many groups have gone a long way toward achieving safe fishing goals in the United States and internationally, including the Environmental Defense Fund, the Natural Resources Defense Council, and Greenpeace. If you don't know where to start, check out any of their websites and decide which issues to put your energy into.

NEW EATING HABITS

Another way to help protect healthy oceans and fish populations is to eat less fish. Try consuming fish less frequently, perhaps only once a week. Here are a few delicious ideas for helping you cut back on fish.

146

- When you're craving fish, try substituting another protein such as tofu, tempeh, beans, eggs, or pasture-raised poultry in its place.
- If it's the briny taste of seafood that you're after, sea vegetables have a similar flavor and can be surprisingly hearty. Paired with crème fraîche and chives, minced hijiki seasoned with vinegar and shoyu makes a tasty stand-in for caviar. Wakame, arame, and dulse give a rich texture to sea vegetable gumbo. Toasted nori is as crisp and light as the bonito flakes that accompany many Japanese dishes, giving a savory exclamation point to salads and starches, with a dramatic black color that makes a striking garnish. Coarsely mashed chickpeas with lemon juice, scallions, and mayonnaise, sprinkled with a few nori flakes, makes a delicious sandwich filling with a texture similar to tuna that you can really sink your teeth into.
- Try making fish merely an element of the dish you're serving, as opposed to a hunk of protein that takes the starring role on the plate. For example, prepare broiled mackerel tossed with escarole and pasta; grilled sardines with artichokes on pizza; or a rich anchovy dressing served on a Caesar or puntarelle salad. If you're craving a tuna sandwich, make the amount in the can go twice as far by loading up the sandwich filling with shaved celery, carrots, scallions, and herbs. Along the same lines, make a spread using smoked fish and purée it with mustard, mayo, and dill to serve on bread, crackers, or sliced vegetables, as in the recipe for Smoked Farmed Trout Purée with Cherry Tomatoes (page 153).

With the growing transparency of fish origins and fishing practices, making responsible seafood choices is easy. Use the ideas above and the many resources available online to make simple adjustments to your diet.

Blueberry Chocolate Decadence Smoothie

This drink is heavenly in the summer, when fresh blueberries are abundant. The bright flavor of blueberries and the earthy taste of chocolate perfectly complement each other, and both are chock-full of antioxidants. Make this recipe with any kind of milk (my favorite is almond milk—see page 73). Makes approximately 4 cups

2 cups fresh blueberries, stemmed, plus more for garnish

1 tablespoon plus 1 teaspoon cocoa powder

1¹/₂ cups milk

1 teaspoon vanilla extract

¹/₄ teaspoon ground cinnamon

Pinch of ground nutmeg

1 tablespoon maple syrup

1 cup ice

Place all of the ingredients in a blender and blend until smooth. Serve immediately. Garnish with extra blueberries, if desired. *(Pictured on page 149, top center)*

Watermelon, Apple, and Lime Shake

This drink is best in the summertime, when watermelons are at their sweetest and most flavorful. For cooling off and rehydrating on a hot day, there is simply nothing better. Because watermelons are huge, relatively inexpensive, and have a high water content, they make a good base for drinks. Experiment with using different varieties of tart and sweet apples. Makes 5 to 6 cups

6 cups coarsely chopped seeded watermelon

2 apples, cored and coarsely chopped

1 tablespoon freshly squeezed lime juice, or more to taste

1 cup ice

Blend 1 cup of the watermelon in a blender until liquid. Add the rest of the watermelon, the apples, lime juice, and ice, and blend until smooth. Taste and add more lime, if desired. *(Pictured on page 149, bottom left)*

Lemonade with Lemon Balm and Lemon Verbena

This recipe was inspired by a visit to the Middle East. The day was hot and dry, and someone gave me lemonade with basil and mint. I have been putting herbs in tea and lemonade ever since. Although you can experiment using all sorts of different fresh herbs, this combination makes for a relaxing tonic, as both lemon balm and lemon verbena are known for their calming properties. On a warm night, substitute this lemonade for a glass of white wine, or turn it into a cocktail by adding white wine or champagne. **Makes approximately 5 cups**

6 fresh lemon balm leaves

4 fresh lemon verbena leaves

Juice of 4 lemons, plus 1 thinly sliced lemon

4 cups water

Honey or organic dry sugar to taste

Pinch of salt

Combine all of the ingredients except the lemon slices in a blender, starting with a modest amount of sweetener. Blend until the herbs are pulverized, about 5 seconds, then taste and adjust the sweetness.

Chill for an hour, or serve immediately over ice, garnished with a slice of lemon. The lemonade is best drunk within two days. *(Pictured opposite, far right)*

Tahini and Honey over Fresh Fruit

This makes for an easy, satisfying breakfast when summer fruit is plentiful. Tahini, a Middle Eastern nut butter made from ground sesame seeds, is most often used to make hummus and baba ghanoush. I find that locally made, organic brands of tahini are fresher, sweeter, and looser than commercial brands, in which the oil has often separated from the solids. **Serves 4**

1 cup tahini	4 cups sliced fresh fruit (berries, peaches, apricots, apples, bananas)
¹/₂ cup honey	

In a small bowl, whisk together the tahini and honey. Divide the fruit among the bowls and top with a heaping ¹/₄ cup of the tahini mixture. Stir gently to incorporate.

Grilled Apricots with Goat Cheese and Balsamic Vinegar

Apricots seem exotic and rare because they disappear from the market before peaches and plums, their stone fruit cousins. Light grilling keeps their pleasing shape intact, and the fruit's natural sweetness is accentuated by the fat and sourness of the goat cheese. If you don't have a grill, sear the apricots in a pan, following the same instructions for grilling. For a sweeter take on this recipe, reduce the salt and pepper and, after topping the apricots with the goat cheese, drizzle them with honey and garnish with a few mint leaves. Serves 4 to 6 as a starter

1/2 cup fresh goat cheese	Salt and freshly ground black pepper
6 ripe apricots	2 tablespoons balsamic vinegar
3 tablespoons olive oil	

Remove the goat cheese from its package, place in a bowl, and let sit at room temperature to soften.

Cut the apricots in half along the seam that runs around the fruit; the two halves should come apart cleanly after you cut all the way around. Remove the pit. Drizzle the halves lightly with the olive oil and season with salt and pepper.

Heat the grill. Place a few apricots on the grill, cut side down, and grill for just under a minute. As you grill, press down firmly with tongs for a couple of seconds to form grill marks. Turn and cook for 10 seconds on the second side. Repeat with the remaining apricots.

Add a dash of water to the goat cheese and stir until it's pliable. Using two spoons, place a generous spoonful of goat cheese in the indentation of each apricot; scoop the cheese with the first one and use the second to push the cheese onto the fruit. Spoon a few drops of the balsamic vinegar over the apricots and season with more pepper. Serve immediately.

Smoked Farmed Trout Purée
with Cherry Tomatoes

A fresh take on the deli favorite, smoked whitefish salad, this version is full of herbs and dressed up by sweet cherry tomatoes. Smoked fish is salty, so you may not need to salt the purée. The fillets contain tiny bones, but as a general rule, the smallest ones are soft and edible. Rainbow or golden trout farmed in the United States is a recommended seafood choice because unlike many carnivorous farmed fish—which eat more protein than they provide to humans—trout efficiently convert their feed into protein. What's more, rainbow and golden trout are mostly farm-raised in tanks, so there is little risk of them contaminating wild populations. **Serves 4 to 6**

$1/2$ cup mayonnaise

$1/4$ cup Dijon mustard

1 cup loosely packed minced fresh dill

1 cup loosely packed minced fresh flat-leaf parsley leaves

4 scallions, green parts only, minced

4 teaspoons freshly squeezed lemon juice

Salt and freshly ground black pepper

$1/2$ pound smoked rainbow or golden trout, skinned and boned

Crackers, bread, or thinly sliced vegetables for serving

1 pint cherry tomatoes, quartered

Place the mayonnaise and mustard in a small bowl with the dill, parsley, and scallions, setting aside 1 tablespoon of each of the herbs for garnish. Add the lemon juice and a few grinds of pepper. Stir and set aside.

Grind the trout in a food processor for 10 seconds, until completely broken down. Transfer the fish to a large bowl and fold in the mayonnaise. Taste and adjust the seasoning, if necessary.

To serve, spread the purée on crackers and scatter the tomatoes over the top. Season with salt and pepper and garnish with a sprinkling of the reserved minced herbs.

Marinated Mackerel with Dill and Horseradish Cream

This lightly pickled mackerel is "cooked" through by the acid in the vinegar. Use high-quality fish, and keep it refrigerated until you marinate it. Use a glass or ceramic baking dish as metal can interfere with the pickling process. Both Spanish and king mackerel are fished using low-impact methods, and populations in the Atlantic and the U.S. Gulf of Mexico are thriving. They reproduce in high numbers and mature quickly, so mackerel are considered safe from overfishing. Start this recipe the night before serving so the fish has time to marinate. Serves 6 to 8 as a starter

2 small Atlantic mackerel about, 3/4 pound each, filleted and pin bones removed

Salt and freshly ground black pepper

4 shallots, thinly sliced

1 (750-ml) bottle dry white wine

1/2 cup white wine vinegar

2 tablespoons honey

1 tablespoon black peppercorns

2 tablespoons dried coriander seeds

1 teaspoon juniper berries

2 bay leaves

1 cup sour cream or crème fraîche

1 cup minced fresh dill

1/4 cup prepared horseradish

Toast points or crackers for serving

Rinse the mackerel fillets and pat them dry. Lay the fillets in a glass or ceramic baking dish, skin side down, and season with salt.

In a saucepan, combine the shallots, wine, vinegar, honey, peppercorns, coriander seeds, juniper berries, bay leaves and 2 tablespoons salt. Bring to a boil. Decrease the heat to medium and simmer, uncovered, for 5 minutes.

Turn off the heat and pour the hot liquid over the mackerel. Cover tightly and let cool to room temperature, then refrigerate overnight.

Put the sour cream in a large bowl. Set aside a few tablespoons of the dill for garnish, and fold in the remaining dill and horseradish. Season with salt and pepper.

To serve, drain the mackerel. Break off pieces of mackerel and place them on the toast points. Arrange the toast on a platter. Season with salt and pepper, and spoon a little of the sour cream mixture onto each toast point. Scatter the reserved dill over the top. After marinating, the mackerel can last 1 day in the refrigerator.

Indonesian Corn Fritters

Galangal is a root that looks like ginger but has a sweet, perfumed taste. Find it fresh (the best choice), frozen, or powdered in Asian markets or gourmet food stores. The citrusy herb lemongrass can be grown from a store-bought stalk; place it in water on the windowsill until it sprouts before transferring it to a pot with soil. These rich fritters need a sweet, tangy sauce; if you don't have time to make Tamarind Ketchup as the recipe calls for, use the simple Cilantro-Jalapeño Sauce (page 184), or whisk store-bought ketchup with honey, lime juice, and salt. Makes approximately 15 fritters

1 stalk lemongrass, root and top half of stem removed

2 tablespoons minced fresh ginger

1 tablespoon galangal, peeled and coarsely chopped

2 shallots, coarsely chopped

3 ears fresh corn, shucked

Salt

1 egg, lightly beaten

1/2 cup flour

Olive oil for frying

Tamarind Ketchup (page 178) or a store-bought tamarind sauce

1 scallion, green part only, thinly sliced for garnish

Bruise the lemongrass with the handle of a chef's knife until the skin splits and the juice begins to seep out. Slice off the root and the papery top third of the stem and discard. Coarsely chop the lemongrass and place in the bowl of a food processor with the ginger, galangal, and shallots. Process until the fibrous lemongrass is completely broken down. You will need to stop and scrape down the sides of the bowl four or five times.

Cut the kernels from the corn. Add 1 cup of the corn kernels to the food processor and grind with the herbs to form a paste. Transfer the paste to a bowl and stir in 4 teaspoons of salt and the rest of the corn kernels. Taste the batter and adjust the seasoning, then stir in the egg. Fold in the flour with a spatula. Let the mixture rest in the refrigerator for 10 minutes.

Set a wire rack over a baking sheet for draining the fritters. Heat a skillet and pour in 1/2 inch of oil. When the oil begins to shimmer, drop in several spoonfuls of the batter, about 2 tablespoons of batter at a time, and fry for 1 minute. Flip and continue frying until golden, about 1 minute more.

Remove with a slotted spoon and drain on the rack. Season with salt.

Serve the fritters immediately with ketchup and garnish with the scallion greens.

Puntarelles with Anchovy Dressing

Puntarelles (shown opposite) are a bitter green used in Italian cuisine, particularly in Rome, where they are served with a dressing of anchovies, garlic, and olive oil. Before eating, soak the puntarelles in ice water for at least 1 hour or up to 12 hours. The longer they soak, the more the bitterness mellows, and the stems become crisp and curly. The strong flavors of the anchovies and garlic, along with the fat from the olive oil, evoke a surprising sweetness from the puntarelles. The overall flavor is similar to that of a Caesar salad, but with a deep, earthy note from the dark greens. Try this salad with the Tortilla Española (page 36) for a beautiful summer meal with Mediterranean flavors. **Serves 4**

1 bunch puntarelles

2 large cloves garlic, peeled

2 anchovy fillets

$1/4$ teaspoon lemon zest

2 tablespoons freshly squeezed lemon juice

2 tablespoons olive oil

2 teaspoons Dijon mustard

Salt and freshly ground black pepper

Cut the stems off the puntarelles and set the leaves aside. Slice the stems thinly lengthwise and place them in a bowl of ice water. Gently agitate the stems to remove any dirt and set them aside. Slice the leaves crosswise into strips $1/2$ inch wide. Add them to the ice water with the stems, agitate, and set aside in the refrigerator for 1 to 12 hours.

To make the dressing, place the garlic and anchovies in a mortar and grind them with a pestle until they are broken down into a paste. Transfer to a large bowl and add the lemon zest and juice, olive oil, mustard, and a dash of salt. Whisk to combine.

Lift the puntarelles out of the ice water, leaving any dirt behind, and dry them in a salad spinner. Toss the puntarelles with the dressing.

Season with black pepper and serve immediately.

Chicken Paillards with Sun-Dried Tomato Purée over Arugula

A paillard is a piece of meat that has been pounded thin and seared. The purée in this recipe is fragrant and colorful, with a powerful tomatoey tang. Leftover purée can be used as a dip for vegetables or tossed with pasta. Do not reuse any purée that came in contact with the raw chicken without first boiling it for one minute. Start this recipe early in the day to allow the tomatoes and nuts enough time to soak. **Serves 4**

$^1/_2$ cup dry-packed sun-dried tomatoes	$^1/_2$ cup olive oil
$^3/_4$ cup freshly squeezed orange juice	1 teaspoon balsamic vinegar
$^1/_2$ cup raw cashews	1 pound arugula leaves
2 cloves garlic, minced	2 skinless, boneless chicken breasts, rinsed and patted dry
1 tablespoon fresh thyme leaves	
	Salt and freshly ground black pepper

Soak the tomatoes in the orange juice for 2 hours. Drain, reserving the juice, and set aside. Meanwhile, soak the cashews in water to cover for 1 hour. Drain. Put the cashews, garlic, and thyme in a food processor and coarsely grind. Add the tomatoes and purée. Add the orange juice and process. With the machine running, pour in 3 tablespoons of the olive oil.

To make the dressing, in a large bowl, whisk 1 tablespoon of the purée with the vinegar and 2 tablespoons of the olive oil. Set aside.

Slice the chicken breasts in half widthwise to make 4 thin fillets. Lay the fillets between 2 slices of parchment paper and pound with a mallet or the bottom of a heavy pan until $^1/_4$ inch thick. Season with salt and pepper and spread a thin layer of purée on each side. Heat a sauté pan over high heat and add the remaining 3 tablespoons oil. Working in batches, sear the paillards for 2 to 3 minutes per side. They should be removed from the heat when the center just turns opaque. Deglaze the pan with $^1/_4$ cup water. Bring the liquid to a boil and whisk to make a sauce. Add a little purée to thicken if needed.

To serve, toss the arugula with the dressing and divide among four plates. Place a piece of warm chicken on each pile of arugula and spoon the pan sauce over the top.

Chilled Cucumber Soup with Avocado, Cumin, and Mint

The peel of the cucumber gives this soup its vibrant green color. Because it's so easy to prepare, assemble all the ingredients beforehand so you can blend the soup just minutes before serving; the flavors will be fresh and the color bright. Don't let it sit for more than 30 minutes or it will lose its luster! **Serves 4**

3 large unwaxed cucumbers	1/2 jalapeño, seeds and ribs removed
1 ripe avocado	1 scallion, green and white parts, coarsely chopped
1/2 cup toasted almonds, plus chopped almonds for garnish	
Juice of 1 lime	1 handful fresh mint leaves
2 teaspoons ground cumin	4 ice cubes
	Salt

Halve the cucumbers lengthwise and scoop out and discard the seeds. Place the cucumbers in a blender. Slice open the avocado. Stick a chef's knife into the pit and twist to remove. Scoop the avocado flesh into the blender. Add the almonds, lime juice, cumin, jalapeño, scallion, and mint. Blend with the ice cubes and 2 cups cold water until smooth. Taste and season with salt.

Serve in glasses garnished with a few chopped almonds.

Watermelon Gazpacho

This sweet and tangy cold soup is one of Lucid Food's signature dishes. For catered events, we often serve it in shot glasses as an hors d'oeuvre. A guest once suggested we top them off with vodka, and so a wonderful new take on the Bloody Mary was invented. You can make this recipe a day ahead and reseason it just before serving. **Serves 4**

6 cups coarsely chopped seeded watermelon

5 ripe tomatoes, cored and quartered

1 rounded tablespoon sweet smoked paprika

1 clove garlic, smashed

$1/2$ cup whole toasted almonds

3 tablespoons balsamic vinegar

1 teaspoon chipotle sauce

Salt

$1/4$ sweet white or red onion, finely diced

1 cucumber, seeded and diced

Blend 2 cups of the watermelon in a blender until liquid. Add the rest of the watermelon, the tomatoes, paprika, garlic, almonds, balsamic vinegar, and chipotle sauce and blend until smooth. Transfer the soup to a bowl and taste and season with salt.

Chill for an hour before serving. Garnish with a spoonful of the onion and cucumber dice.

Heirloom Beans

Look for heirloom beans to substitute for all kinds of beans in Chunky Tortilla Soup and other recipes. In Mexican cooking, most of us are familiar only with pinto and black beans, but there are countless varieties of beans indigenous to the Americas that are as easy to prepare and often better tasting, not to mention fresher than the beans on supermarket shelves, which can be several years old.

We no longer have easy access to heirloom beans, since the advent of centralized agriculture means that it became more profitable to sell a small number of beans that look uniform and have high yields. But the beans most easily available to us are not necessarily the best tasting. Savory Mexican beans that you may not have heard of include Vallartas, Negro Criollo de Hidalgos, and Ayote Morados (Purple Runners). You can find heirloom beans online. There are several purveyors and organizations dedicated to preserving heirlooms listed in the Resources section (page 193), or find them in specialty food stores and at farmers' markets. If we create a demand for them, these largely forgotten treasures will come back to the market and flourish. If you have a garden, try planting some at home.

Chunky Tortilla Soup

This rustic soup is laden with beans, vegetables, and cheese. A chunky version of the typically smooth tortilla soup, it doesn't require any traditional soup stock; the tomato juice and sweet corn cobs make a rich broth full of the fresh, south-of-the-border tastes of summertime. Read about incorporating heirloom beans into dishes like this one on the opposite page. Serves 4

Three 6-inch round corn tortillas

3 tablespoons olive oil

5 ripe tomatoes

1 yellow onion, minced

1½ cups cooked black beans

3 ears fresh corn, kernels removed and cobs reserved

1 clove garlic, minced

2 teaspoons chile powder

Salt and freshly ground black pepper

1 cup crumbled queso fresco

1 ripe avocado, pitted, peeled, and thinly sliced

Leaves from 1 bunch fresh cilantro, coarsely chopped

2 limes, quartered

1 jalapeño, seeded and thinly sliced

Preheat the oven to 400°F. Line a baking sheet with parchment paper.

Cut the tortillas in half, then into ½-inch strips. Place the strips in a bowl and toss with 1 tablespoon of the olive oil, then spread them on the baking sheet. Bake until crisp, 8 to 10 minutes. Set aside.

Position a fine-mesh strainer over a large bowl. Core and halve the tomatoes and scoop out the seeds, holding them over the strainer so all of the juice falls into the bowl. Press the seeds with a ladle to extract as much juice as possible. Discard the seeds and set the juice aside. Dice the tomatoes.

Heat a soup pot and add the remaining 2 tablespoons olive oil. Add the onion and sauté until soft, then stir in the tomatoes, black beans, corn kernels, garlic, and chile powder. Add the tomato juice, 3 cups water, and corn cobs. If your pot is small, break the cobs in half so they fit. Bring to a boil, then decrease the heat and simmer, uncovered, for 10 minutes. Remove the corn cobs. Season with salt and pepper.

Serve the soup topped with several tortilla strips, ¼ cup queso fresco, a few avocado slices, and a small handful of cilantro. Serve the lime and jalapeño slices on the side.

Stuffed Poblano Chile Peppers

These poblanos are stuffed with tempeh, a traditional Indonesian food made from fermented soybeans. Tempeh tastes rich and meaty when seasoned and cooked properly. The chiles can be either grilled or roasted. You can prepare the filling and even stuff the chiles the night before cooking. For a memorable summer meal, serve with Pickled Mango and Habanero Relish or Mango and Habanero Salsa Cruda (page 183) and grilled corn on the cob. **Makes 8 stuffed poblanos**

2 tablespoons olive oil, plus more as needed

1 yellow onion, diced

1 bunch kale, stems removed and finely chopped

8 ounces plain tempeh, crumbled

1 tablespoon ground cumin

1 tablespoon plus 2 teaspoons chile powder

1 teaspoon ground cloves

3 cloves garlic, minced

2 tablespoons soy sauce

1 tablespoon honey

2 cups crumbled queso fresco

Salt

8 poblano chile peppers

To make the filling, heat a large sauté pan over medium-high heat and add 2 tablespoons olive oil. Add the onion and sauté until it begins to brown, then stir in the kale and cook until just wilted, about 2 minutes. Add the tempeh, cumin, chile powder, and cloves. Cook for 1 minute. Add the garlic, soy sauce, honey, and ½ cup water and simmer, stirring frequently, for 5 minutes. Turn off the heat and let cool to room temperature. Stir in the queso fresco and season with salt.

To prepare the chiles, slice off the stem end of each one so you have a wide hole for stuffing. Using a sharp knife, reach inside and slice out the membranes and seeds. Work carefully so as not to puncture the skin.

Preheat the oven to 425°F, or preheat the grill to medium.

Rub the chiles inside and out with olive oil. Using a small spoon to pack the narrow end, stuff the chiles with the filling. Pack them as tightly as possible without tearing the flesh. This will help to hold the stuffing in during cooking.

If roasting, put the chiles in a lightly greased casserole dish, cover, and roast for 5 minutes. Uncover and roast for 10 minutes more. Rotate the chiles in the pan so a different side is facing up, and roast for another 10 minutes, or until the poblano skin is lightly charred and the filling is heated through. If grilling, place the chiles directly over the heat and cook for about 15 minutes, rotating two or three times. Serve hot.

Grilled Pizza

When making grilled pizza, roll the dough very thin so that it cooks through quickly. This means that it'll burn easily, so keep an eye on the dough as it cooks. If you're new to grilling pizza, make an extra batch of dough, in case a few pizzas get sacrificed to the gods of grilling. Apply toppings lightly—just a few tablespoons each. Makes six 12- to 14-inch pizzas

2 tablespoons fresh yeast or 2 teaspoons active dry yeast	¹/₄ cup olive oil, plus more as needed
1 tablespoon organic white sugar	Assorted spreads and toppings (see opposite)
5 cups flour, plus more for kneading	Salt and freshly ground black pepper
Salt	Red pepper flakes (optional)

Crumble the yeast in a small bowl. Add ¹/₂ cup warm water and the sugar, and stir with your fingers to dissolve the yeast. Set the bowl in a warm place until the yeast starts to foam and bubble, about 5 minutes.

Put the flour in a large bowl, and stir in 4 teaspoons of salt. Make a hole in the flour and pour in the yeast, 1 cup plus 2 tablespoons water, and the olive oil. Coat your hands with oil and mix until you have a uniform dough.

Turn the dough onto a floured board and knead for 5 minutes. Transfer to a bowl and drizzle with olive oil. Cover with a damp cloth and put the bowl in a warm place until the dough doubles in size, 60 to 80 minutes.

Divide the dough into 6 pieces and roll each into a ball. Cover with a damp cloth and put them in a warm place to rise for 45 minutes.

On a lightly floured board, roll the balls out into flat discs no more than ¹/₄ inch thick. Stack the discs on a baking sheet between layers of parchment paper and store in the refrigerator until you're about to grill.

Heat the grill to a medium-high temperature, and rub it with an old dish towel dipped in olive oil. Assemble the toppings and position them close to the grill.

Brush a disc of dough with olive oil and drop it on the grill, oiled side down. Brush the top with oil and season with salt. Grill for 2 to 3 minutes. Use a metal spatula or tongs to gently move different parts of the dough onto the grill's hot spot. The dough will bubble up as it cooks. Using tongs, peer underneath to check the color. When the bottom looks evenly toasted, flip the dough. Immediately sprinkle on the cheese if using, followed by the other toppings. Close the lid for 30 seconds to melt the cheese. Open the cover and continue grilling until the crust is brown and marked with grill marks, 2 to 3 minutes. Take the pizza off the grill and rub the grill with the oiled dish towel. Repeat with the remaining dough and toppings.

Serve immediately with salt, pepper, and red pepper flakes if using.

Pizza Toppings: The Sky's the Limit

Making your own pizza is fun and creative, especially in the summer, when there are so many fresh ingredients available. For the toppings, use any combination of cooked or raw vegetables, shredded or crumbled cheese, sauce, and herbs. Recipes from this book that make great toppings include: Stinging Nettle Pesto (page 115); Smoky Eggplant Dip with Yogurt (page 192); Watercress Mashed Potatoes (page 185); and Chicken Paillards with Sun-Dried Tomato Purée (page 158). There are also many vegetable dishes that work beautifully on pizza: Grilled Maitake Mushrooms (page 40); Fava Beans and Seared Zucchini (page 123); Baby Artichokes with Fresh Chervil (page 116); and Sautéed Leafy Greens (page 186). Choose from cheeses such as mozzarella, ricotta, fontina, or Gruyère.

Sustainable Seafood Choice: Farmed Mussels

Mussel farming is an exemplary sustainable operation due entirely to the nature of the animals. Mussels do not need fishmeal or fish oil in their diets but instead nourish themselves by drawing seawater through their gills and retaining the tiny plants and animals known as plankton. Mussels are not prone to contagion, so antibiotics and chemicals are not needed to maintain a disease-free population. In fact, mussel farming often *improves* water quality because mussels cannot live in polluted water. Farm owners thus have a vested interest in keeping the surrounding coastal waters clean.

Grilled Mussels with Simmered Tomatoes over Couscous

I tasted grilled mussels for the first time last summer and they were a revelation. Grilled mussels cook in their own brine and have a rich, undiluted flavor. This Mediterranean-style meal pairs them with fluffy couscous and a quick tomato sauce. This recipe also works beautifully with clams. You can cook the tomatoes a day ahead and warm them up just before serving.
Serves 4 to 6

8 tomatoes, quartered	¹/₂ cup white wine
2 tablespoons olive oil, plus more for drizzling	2 cups Israeli couscous
	Salt and freshly ground black pepper
1 yellow onion, diced	2 pounds farmed mussels
4 cloves garlic, minced	1 bunch fresh flat-leaf parsley, coarsely chopped for garnish
5 sprigs fresh oregano	

Position a fine-mesh strainer over a bowl. Holding the tomatoes over the strainer, scoop out the seeds, letting the juice and seeds fall into the strainer. Press the seeds with a ladle to extract as much juice as possible. Discard the seeds and set the juice aside. Halve the tomato quarters and set them aside.

Heat the oil in a large skillet over medium-high heat. Add the onion and sauté for 5 minutes. Stir in the tomatoes, garlic, and oregano. Add the wine and tomato juice and bring to a boil. Decrease the heat and boil gently, uncovered, for 12 minutes. Remove from the heat. Set the tomato mixture aside, covered.

Put the couscous in a saucepan with 1 teaspoon salt. Bring 2¹/₂ cups water to a boil and pour it over the couscous. Cover and simmer for 10 minutes, stirring occasionally. Turn off the heat and let it rest, covered, for 5 minutes. Fluff with a fork, then cover and set aside.

Just before cooking, clean the mussels. Gently tap any open shells against a countertop and wait a minute for the shell to close. If the shell stays open, the mussel is dead and must be discarded. Remove the little thistle of fiber, called the beard, that sticks out of the shell by yanking it toward the narrow end of the mussel. Fill a large bowl halfway with cold water and stir in a handful of salt. Soak the mussels in the water for 30 minutes, then lift them out, leaving the debris behind, and set them in a colander.

Heat a grill and place the mussels between the grates. Grill until the mussels are open and cooked through, about 6 minutes.

To serve, put a scoop of couscous on a plate, followed by the tomatoes, then the mussels. Season with salt, pepper, and a dash of olive oil. Garnish with the parsley.

Tofu Banh Mi Sandwiches

Banh mi sandwiches are a Vietnamese street food. Instead of the typical pork and mayonnaise, this version features baked tofu, an anchovy-miso dressing, and cucumber pickles. A key element of banh mi sandwiches is fresh bread—day-old bread is too dry. The best bread to use is a thin-crust white flour baguette that won't overwhelm the sandwich fillings. Try making these sandwiches for a July picnic. **Serves 4**

Olive oil for greasing

14 ounces extra-firm tofu, drained and sliced crosswise ¹/₄ inch thick

Salt and freshly ground black pepper

MARINADE

3 anchovy fillets

2 cloves garlic

2 tablespoons honey

2 tablespoons mirin

2 tablespoons sweet white miso

2 tablespoons Dijon mustard

Salt

¹/₄ cup olive oil

PICKLES

2 kirby cucumbers, halved lengthwise, seeded, and cut into ¹/₄-inch half moons

¹/₂ cup white vinegar

2 tablespoons honey

1 star anise

1 teaspoon salt

1 fresh baguette

Leaves from 1 small handful fresh cilantro

Leaves from 1 small handful fresh mint

1 fresh jalapeño, seeded and thinly sliced

Preheat the oven to 350°F. Lightly grease a baking sheet with olive oil.

Arrange the tofu slices on the baking sheet and season with salt.

To make the marinade, in a blender combine the anchovies, garlic, honey, mirin, miso, and mustard. Add a dash of salt and blend for 30 seconds. With the machine running, slowly pour in the olive oil and blend until smooth.

Rub ¹/₂ teaspoon of the marinade into the top of each tofu slice and bake for 20 minutes. Flip the slices, rub the second side with marinade, and bake for 20 minutes more. Remove from the oven and let cool.

To make the pickles, put the cucumber slices in a small bowl. Whisk together the vinegar, honey, star anise, and salt in a small saucepan and bring to a boil. Pour the vinegar mixture over the cucumbers. Let cool.

To assemble the sandwiches, cut the baguette into 4 pieces. Slice open each piece and generously spread both sides with the marinade. Put 2 to 3 slices of tofu in each sandwich and add a few pinches of cilantro and mint leaves. Season with salt and pepper. Tuck in a few pickles and jalapeño slices and serve.

Apricot Shortcake with Lavender Whipped Cream

Start this recipe the night before serving it so that the lavender can soak in the cream and impart a strong flavor. Use fresh or dried lavender, but stay away from ornamental lavender, which is usually treated with pesticides. If you prefer, substitute peaches or nectarines for the apricots. **Serves 8**

WHIPPED CREAM

2 cups heavy cream

1 tablespoon fresh or dried lavender buds

2 tablespoons honey

BISCUITS

1/2 cup honey

2 eggs

1/2 cup whole raw almonds

1 tablespoon fresh or dried lavender buds

2 cups flour, plus more for shaping biscuits

1 tablespoon baking powder

Pinch of salt

5 tablespoons cold unsalted butter, cut into 1/4-inch pieces, plus 1 tablespoon unsalted butter, melted

APRICOT FILLING

10 ripe apricots, pitted and cut into 1-inch slices

2 teaspoons freshly squeezed lemon juice

3 tablespoons honey

To make the whipped cream, pour the cream into a bowl and stir in the lavender. Cover and refrigerate overnight.

Preheat the oven to 375°F. Oil a baking sheet and line it with parchment paper.

To make the biscuits, whisk together the honey and eggs in a small bowl and set aside. Place the almonds, lavender, flour, baking powder, and salt in a food processor and grind to a coarse powder. Add the cold butter and pulse for 15 seconds. Transfer to a bowl and pour the egg mixture over the top. Mix just until the dough comes together, and refrigerate for 10 minutes.

Pack the dough to just below the top of a 1/3-cup measuring cup, then invert and tap out onto the baking sheet. Repeat to make 8 biscuits total. Brush the discs with the melted butter and bake for 15 minutes. Rotate the pan and bake until the biscuits are golden on top, about 5 minutes more. Transfer to a wire rack and let cool.

Strain the cream, discarding the lavender buds, and whip it until it forms soft peaks. While whipping slowly, gradually add the honey and whip to incorporate.

To make the filling, toss the apricots with the lemon juice and maple syrup.

To serve, halve the biscuits. Spoon the apricot pieces on the bottom half, top with cream, and cover with the top half of the biscuit.

Fresh Berry Dessert Sauce

This is a quick sauce that's not overly sweet. Serve it over cake, ice cream, or yogurt. Straw-berries, mulberries, blackberries, raspberries, and boysenberries will all work well, either on their own or mixed. For a piquant sauce, be sure to use sweet, full-flavored berries. Makes 1¹/₂ cups sauce

2 cups fresh berries, washed, stemmed, and coarsely chopped	1 tablespoon balsamic vinegar
	¹/₂ teaspoon vanilla extract
2 tablespoons maple syrup	8 grinds of freshly ground black pepper

Combine all the ingredients in the bowl of a food processor and pulse about 10 times. The sauce should be coarse, with small chunks of berries. Chill for 30 minutes before serving so the flavors can marry. The sauce is best used within 24 hours.

Fresh Fruit Sorbet

You can make sorbet by simply freezing fruit and pushing it through a juicer. That's it. While plain fruit in season is quite sweet on its own, you can top the sorbet with maple syrup or any other sweetener of your choice. Toppings could include chopped nuts, cacao nibs, or whipped cream. If the fruit freezes for more than an hour, it be will be too hard, and you will need to thaw it a bit before it can pass smoothly through the juicer. Serves 4

1¹/₂ pounds (about 6 cups sliced) fresh fruit, such as strawberries, blackberries, raspberries, peaches, cherimoyas, guavas, papaya, and bananas, stemmed and seeded

If necessary, cut the fruit into pieces 1 inch wide so the pieces will fit easily into the funnel of the juicer. Line a baking sheet with parchment paper, and spread the fruit on the baking sheet. Freeze for 1 hour.

Set up a juicing machine and push the fruit through the funnel. Serve the sorbet immediately.

Blueberry Cobbler
with Oat Scone Topping

In summer, look for blueberries on hikes in temperate parts of the country. Last summer, I found enough for an entire pie on a hike in upstate New York. Wild blueberries can be even sweeter than farmers' market berries, while store-bought berries can have high pesticide residues. So if you get the chance to pick them yourself, you might end up with a healthier and tastier cobbler. Serve with good-quality vanilla ice cream. **Serves 8**

SCONE TOPPING

³/₄ cup rolled oats

³/₄ cup flour

Pinch of salt

1 tablespoon baking powder

¹/₂ teaspoon ground cinnamon

¹/₄ teaspoon ground nutmeg

¹/₄ cup cold unsalted butter, cut into ¹/₄-inch pieces, plus 1 tablespoon unsalted butter, melted

1 egg, lightly beaten

¹/₄ cup brown rice syrup (see page 68)

FILLING

3 pints blueberries

2 tablespoons freshly squeezed lemon juice

1 tablespoon vanilla extract

¹/₂ cup brown rice syrup (see page 68)

Pinch of salt

Preheat the oven to 375°F. Butter a 10-inch pie dish.

To make the topping, grind the oats in a food processor for 30 seconds. Set aside 2 tablespoons of the ground oats in a large bowl. Add the flour, salt, baking powder, cinnamon, and nutmeg to the food processor and process until the ingredients are mixed. Add the cold butter and process until the pieces are pea-size or smaller. Transfer to a bowl. In a separate small bowl, whisk together the egg and brown rice syrup. Pour the wet ingredients into the dry and mix just until the dough comes together.

To make the filling, add the blueberries to the 2 tablespoons of reserved oats. Add the lemon juice, vanilla extract, brown rice syrup, and salt and stir until the berries are coated. Scrape the filling into the pie dish. Crumble the scone topping over the filling, leaving small holes so that the berries can release their steam. Drizzle the topping with the melted butter. Place the pie dish on a baking sheet to catch any drips. Bake for 20 minutes, then rotate the pan and continue baking until the top is golden, about 15 minutes more. Serve hot.

accompaniments

Following are simple pickles, sauces, and side dishes that round out many of the recipes in this book. There is a wide range of flavors to enjoy, including Southeast Asian, Mexican, Mediterranean, and classic American. Some of these foods are seasonal, while others can be made any time of year. As you add these versatile sidekicks to your culinary repertoire, think of the ingredients more as guidelines than as hard-and-fast rules. Get creative and make them your own; there is a lot of room for interpretation.

In this chapter, you'll find basic information to help get you started on pickling and preserving food, and techniques you can use to make preserves, chutneys, and pickles. You can preserve food in jars, also known as canning, any time of year, but the most obvious time is in early fall, when the full spectrum of warm-weather produce is at its peak.

177

Tamarind Ketchup

Tamarind provides acidity with a delicious fruity tartness. It is mainly used in Indian, Thai, and Mexican cooking, although it grows in many tropical climates, including Florida. Look for the caramel-colored tamarind concentrate or paste in markets, as extracting the fruit from the pods is labor-intensive. Use the ketchup on the Indonesian Corn Fritters (page 155), Indian Spiced Scrambled Eggs (page 75), and burgers or grilled shrimp. For all of the preserving recipes, including this one, use kosher salt; unlike table salt, it is free of additives that can discolor ingredients. **Makes 2 cups**

8 ripe tomatoes (preferably Romas)

1 small yellow onion, diced

1 clove garlic, smashed

1 cup honey

1 tablespoon apple cider vinegar

4 teaspoons kosher salt

1 cup golden tamarind concentrate or paste (not dark brown)

1/2 teaspoon whole cloves

1/2 teaspoon allspice

1 cinnamon stick, broken into pieces

Bring a pot of water to a boil, and set up a bowl with ice water. Cut a shallow X in the bottom of each tomato, place them in the boiling water for 45 seconds, and transfer to the ice water. As soon as you can handle them, pull off the skins. Core and halve the tomatoes. Scoop out the seeds over a strainer and press them to extract the juice, then discard the seeds.

Put the tomatoes, their juice, the onion, and garlic in a blender and blend until smooth. Transfer to a large pot and add the honey, vinegar, and salt. Add the tamarind concentrate, passing it through a strainer to remove any stray bits of shell. Tie the cloves, allspice, and cinnamon in a piece of cheesecloth and add them to the pot. Bring to a boil, then decrease the heat and simmer, uncovered, until the ketchup evenly coats the back of a spoon. Let the ketchup cool to room temperature. Remove the cheesecloth bundle and pour into an airtight container and refrigerate for up to 2 months.

Pickled Cauliflower

This is a simple pickle with bold flavors. For a variation, try adding fresh herbs, a dash of red pepper flakes, or a wedge of orange. **Fills 1 pint jar**

2 scant cups cauliflower florets	1¼ cups apple cider vinegar
1 clove garlic, crushed	1 tablespoon honey
½ teaspoon black peppercorns	2 teaspoons kosher salt

Place the cauliflower, garlic, and peppercorns in a sterilized pint jar, leaving ½ inch of headspace at the top of the jar. Place the vinegar, honey, and salt in a small saucepan and bring to a boil, stirring to dissolve the honey and salt. Boil for 1 minute. Pour the hot vinegar into the jar of cauliflower, fully immersing the cauliflower. There may be a little extra pickling liquid left over.

Let cool to room temperature, seal, and refrigerate. The pickles are ready to eat after 3 weeks and will keep in the refrigerator for up to 2 months.

Basic Canning

Canning is a straightforward process that experienced veterans can do instinctively. It's fun and easy, but because detailed procedures must be followed in order to prevent the growth of toxic bacteria, you should first learn from an experienced canner or study one of the books recommended in the Resources section (page 194) if you want to strike out on your own. Describing the full canning process, which results in foods that can be stored at room temperature for up to a year in a cool, dark, place, is beyond the scope of this book, so the preserve recipes that follow are ones that can be stored in the fridge for 1 to 2 months.

Mixed Pickled Vegetables

A pickle can be a symphony of flavors. Be creative with pickling spices—try throwing in the whole kitchen sink if you like. Experiment with different accents: cumin seeds and coriander for an Indian pickle; caraway, celery, and mustard seeds to evoke Eastern European flavors; ginger, garlic, bruised lemongrass, and a shot of soy for a taste of Southeast Asia. For a crisp pickle start with crisp fruits and vegetables; those that are just shy of ripe work well. **Fills 2 pint jars**

3 scant cups cleaned vegetables and fruits, sliced $1/4$ inch thick, such as: red onions; carrots; beets; radishes; cucumber; scallions (trimmed to 2-inch lengths); whole smashed garlic cloves; rutabaga; green tomatoes; unripe mangoes; Fuyu persimmons

2 teaspoons mustard seeds

2 teaspoons coriander seeds

1 teaspoon black peppercorns

2 dried bay leaves

1 teaspoon allspice berries

2 shallots, quartered

Pinch of red pepper flakes

$2^1/_2$ cups white wine vinegar

2 tablespoons honey

4 teaspoons kosher salt

Divide the vegetables, mustard seeds, coriander seeds, peppercorns, bay leaves, allspice, shallots, and red pepper flakes evenly between 2 sanitized pint jars, leaving $1/_2$ inch of headspace at the top of the jar.

In a saucepan, bring the vinegar, honey, and salt to a boil, stirring to dissolve the honey and salt. Boil for 1 minute. Pour the hot vinegar into the jars, fully immersing the vegetables. There may be a little extra pickling liquid left over.

Let cool to room temperature, seal, and refrigerate. The pickles are ready to eat after 2 weeks and will keep in the refrigerator for up to 2 months.

Citrus Chutney

This is the basic procedure for making any fruit chutney. Non-citrus fruits such as peaches, plums, apricots, and mangoes will need to be peeled. Use any citrus fruit combination for this recipe, although you may need to adjust the sweetness for more tart varieties like grapefruit. I chose kumquats and Meyer lemons because I like their contrasting shapes and colors, and both are naturally quite sweet. **Makes 2 cups**

1 cup kumquats, thinly sliced	3/4 cup honey
1 cup diced unpeeled Meyer lemons	1 1/2 teaspoons kosher salt
1/2 cup diced yellow onion	1 tablespoon minced fresh ginger
1/2 cup white wine vinegar	

Place a small dish in the freezer. Combine all of the ingredients with 2 cups water in a pot and bring to a boil. Decrease the heat and cook on a low boil, covered, for 10 minutes. Uncover and bring the chutney back up to a boil. Uncover and increase the heat so the chutney boils rapidly for 20 minutes. Turn off the heat and place a few tablespoons on the frozen dish. Replace the dish in the freezer. After 5 minutes, nudge the chutney with a spoon or your finger. If it has the proper consistency, it's done. If the chutney is still runny, continue to cook for another few minutes, then test it again. To store in the refrigerator, let the chutney cool to room temperature. Pour into an airtight container and refrigerate for up to 2 months.

Variation: Citrus Marmalade

For a delicious, easy marmalade, leave out the onion and vinegar, and use just a dash of salt. The ginger is optional.

Pickled Mango and Habanero Relish

Habaneros are wonderful citrus-infused chiles that come to us from Mexico. If you can't find habaneros, substitute a couple of jalapeño peppers and a splash of orange juice. Habaneros are powerful and will sting badly if accidentally rubbed near the eyes, so always wear gloves when handling them. Serve with the Stuffed Poblano Chile Peppers (page 165). **Makes 2 cups**

1 habanero chile	$^1/_4$ cup honey
$^1/_4$ cup minced yellow onion	$^1/_2$ cup white wine vinegar
2 heaping cups finely diced ripe (but not mushy) mangoes	2 teaspoons salt

Wearing latex or rubber gloves, slice the stem off the habanero. Slice open and, with a sharp knife, remove the membrane and seeds and discard. Mince the habanero. Place in a nonreactive saucepan with all the remaining ingredients and bring to a boil, stirring to dissolve the salt. Decrease the heat and simmer, uncovered, for 5 minutes.

Pour the salsa into an airtight container and let cool to room temperature, then seal and refrigerate. The relish is ready to eat right away and will keep in the refrigerator for up to 1 month.

Variation: Mango and Habanero Salsa Cruda

For quick, fresh, salsa cruda, combine the habanero, 1 white onion (as opposed to yellow), and mango in a bowl with the juice of 1 lime. Taste and adjust the salt as needed, then refrigerate for 1 hour to let the flavors develop. This salsa tastes best within a day of being made.

Cilantro-Jalapeño Sauce

We have Mexico to thank for the tangy flavor combination of cilantro, jalapeño, and lime, although this sauce complements all types of cuisines. Pair it with crispy appetizers like the Chickpea Cakes (page 39) or Indonesian Corn Fritters (page 155), or serve it alongside the Indian Spiced Scrambled Eggs (page 75). Try pouring it over grilled chicken or fish for a zesty finish. Serve this sauce in the first hour after blending, when its color is brightest. **Makes approximately 1 cup**

2 cups fresh cilantro leaves

1 or 2 jalapeños, ribs and seeds removed and coarsely chopped

2 tablespoons honey

3 tablespoons freshly squeezed lime juice

1 tablespoon olive oil

Salt

Combine the cilantro, jalapeño, honey, lime juice, and olive oil in a food processor or blender and blend until liquefied. Taste and season with salt. If you prefer more heat, add another jalapeño and blend again.

Cucumber Yogurt

From Greece to India, a variation of this condiment is a standard accompaniment to most meals. It's a versatile recipe to have in your arsenal, as it lends a light richness to grilled chicken or fish, bean soups, and almost any dish of Mediterranean origin. Try adding a little minced garlic, currants, raisins, fresh dill, or lemon juice. If you can't find fresh mint, use dried. **Makes 2 cups**

1/2 cucumber, peeled, halved, and seeded

5 fresh mint leaves

2 cups plain yogurt

Salt and freshly ground black pepper

Thinly slice the cucumbers and squeeze them to press out the excess water. Mince the mint leaves. In a small bowl, combine the cucumber, mint, and yogurt. Season with salt and pepper.

Watercress Mashed Potatoes

Watercress (shown below) gives these mashed potatoes a peppery bite. They are a perfect accompaniment to fish, chicken, and mushroom entrées. Try serving them with the Grape and Ginger–Glazed Chicken (page 56). If you have leftovers, add hot stock to make a warming soup. Alternatively, whisk in milk or cream and serve as the classic cold potato soup vichyssoise. **Makes approximately 5 cups**

Salt and freshly ground black pepper

1 bunch watercress, coarsely chopped

1 leek, green and white parts, minced

3 tablespoons unsalted butter, at room temperature

4 cups Yukon Gold potatoes, peeled and cut into 1-inch dice

3 tablespoons olive oil

Season a pot of cold water with enough salt so that it tastes like seawater. Bring to a boil, add the watercress and leek, and blanch for 1 minute, then shock in cold water. Using your hands, squeeze out as much water as possible. Pulse the watercress, leek, and butter in a food processor until puréed, 30 seconds to 1 minute.

Put the potatoes in a pot and cover with cold water. Add a dash of salt, bring the water to a boil, and cook until the potatoes are tender when pierced with a fork, about 5 minutes. Drain, and push the potatoes through a ricer or mash them in the pot. Fold in the olive oil, then the puréed watercress and leek. Season with salt and pepper.

Sautéed Leafy Greens

I like to eat leafy greens every day, and this is an easy, delicious way to prepare them. Use any leafy green like kale, collard greens, chard (shown opposite), or beet greens. The cooking time for spinach will be a little shorter. These greens make a great side to most main dishes. Paired with brown rice or quinoa they make a simple, healthy lunch. I like to add an entire bunch of fresh chopped parsley just before the pan comes off the heat. Makes 3 cups

1 bunch leafy greens	2 cloves garlic, minced
2 tablespoons olive oil	Pinch of red pepper flakes (optional)
Salt and freshly ground black pepper	1 tablespoon freshly squeezed lemon juice

Slice out the fibrous inner stem of the greens and discard. Coarsely chop, making sure there are no long strands, and then submerge the greens in cold water. Swish them around with your hands to remove any dirt, then transfer to a colander. Repeat if the greens are very sandy. Make sure to lift the greens out, don't pour them into the colander, or all of the dirt will come out with them. There is no need to dry the greens, because the water clinging to the greens helps in the cooking process.

Heat a large sauté pan over medium-high heat and add the olive oil. Throw in half of the greens, sauté them for 30 seconds until they've shrunk a little, then add the other half. Sauté until the leaves are tender but still bright green, about 3 minutes, adding a dash of salt as you cook. Add the garlic and sauté for 1 minute more. Turn off the heat and stir in the red pepper flakes if you're using them.

Serve hot, seasoned with lemon juice and freshly ground black pepper.

Sweet Potato and Cranberry Cornmeal Biscuits

My contribution to my family's Thanksgiving meal has always been cornbread. In making it so many times, I discovered that it's a great vehicle for fruit, cooked grains, or vegetables. This variation has a thick batter, so these are more like biscuits than bread. Pale orange and scarlet-flecked, these biscuits make a beautiful addition to a holiday table. **Makes 12 biscuits**

1 sweet potato, peeled and coarsely chopped	3 tablespoons maple syrup (see page 69)
1 cup freshly squeezed orange juice	1 cup fresh cranberries
2 teaspoons salt	1 cup cornmeal
5 tablespoons unsalted butter, at room temperature, plus 1 tablespoon melted butter for brushing	1 cup flour
	1 tablespoon baking powder

Preheat the oven to 425°F. Grease a baking sheet or muffin tin and set aside.

Put the sweet potato in a small saucepan with the orange juice, $\frac{1}{2}$ cup water, and 1 teaspoon of the salt. Bring to a boil, then decrease the heat slightly and boil gently, covered, until very soft, about 10 minutes. Coarsely mash the potatoes and cooking liquid with the 5 tablespoons butter and maple syrup. Stir in the cranberries. Let cool and set aside.

In a large bowl, whisk together the cornmeal, flour, baking powder, and the remaining 1 teaspoon salt. Stir in the sweet potatoes. Refrigerate for 1 hour.

To form each biscuit, pack the dough to just below the top of a $\frac{1}{3}$-cup measuring cup, then invert and tap out onto the baking sheet. Repeat to make 12 biscuits total. Brush the top of each biscuit with a little melted butter. Bake for 15 minutes, then rotate and continue baking until the tops are golden and firm, about 5 minutes more. Transfer to a wire rack to cool. Serve warm or cold.

Green Rice

My Iranian father is infamous for knowing how to make one single dish: rice cooked with lentils, dill, and spices. Rice is ubiquitous in Persian cooking, and there are many elaborate variations that include dried fruit, fresh herbs, nuts, and beans. This version is green and aromatic. Dried limes have a distinctly sour, herbal taste specific to Persian food. Whole or powdered dried limes can be found at the stores listed in this book's Resources section (page 193), but if you can't find either one, the rice can be cooked with 2 teaspoons of lemon zest and seasoned with 2 tablespoons of lemon juice right before serving. **Makes 6 cups**

2 cups long-grain basmati rice	1 teaspoon dried lime powder, or 1 preserved whole lime
Salt	
1 teaspoon saffron threads or powder	1 cup minced fresh flat-leaf parsley
3 tablespoons olive oil	1 cup minced fresh cilantro
2 leeks, green and white parts, finely diced	$^1/_3$ cup minced fresh dill
	1 cup shelled, toasted pistachios

Put the rice in a large bowl and cover with cold water. Toss the rice with your hands a few times to remove the starch, and drain. Repeat this process five times. Set aside.

Pour $3^1/_2$ cups water into a small pot with a dash of salt and bring to a boil. Meanwhile, put the saffron in a small bowl with 2 tablespoons of water. Stir and set aside.

Heat a large pot over medium-high heat and add the oil. Add the leeks and sauté for 5 minutes. Add the rice, saffron water, and lime powder or whole preserved lime and cook, stirring often, for 2 minutes. Pour the boiling water over the rice, bring the rice to a boil, then decrease the heat and simmer, covered, for 20 minutes. Turn off the heat and let the rice stand, covered, for 5 minutes, then fluff with a fork. If the whole lime was used, discard.

Transfer the rice to a large bowl and fold in the parsley, cilantro, dill, and most of the pistachios. Season with salt. To serve, pile the rice on a platter and scatter a few pistachios over the top.

Smoky Eggplant Dip with Yogurt

Start this recipe the night before you serve it if you are straining the yogurt. To convert one cup of regular yogurt to ¹/₂ cup of thick Greek-style yogurt, set a strainer over a bowl and line it with a clean, lint-free dish towel or a coffee filter and pour in one cup of yogurt. Put the bowl in the refrigerator overnight. The next day, discard the liquid and scrape the thickened yogurt into a bowl. Serve this dip with bread or raw vegetables, or as part of a Middle Eastern spread with Cucumber Yogurt (page 184), Cucumber and Pomegranate Salad (page 85), and Chickpea Cakes (page 39). Makes approximately 2 cups

1 medium-size globe eggplant	¹/₄ cup plus 2 tablespoons olive oil
1 clove garlic, minced	¹/₄ cup fresh flat-leaf parsley leaves
2 tablespoons freshly squeezed lemon juice	Salt and freshly ground black pepper
¹/₂ cup Greek-style yogurt, or 1 cup regular yogurt, drained overnight	Dash of paprika

Turn a gas burner on high and use tongs to place the eggplant directly on the burner. Char the eggplant, turning it once every minute or so, until it is evenly charred, black, and tender, about 6 minutes. Remove from the flame and let cool in a strainer or colander set over a bowl. If you don't have a gas stove, poke holes in the eggplant with a fork and cook on a greased baking sheet in a 400°F oven until soft, 30 to 40 minutes. Let cool.

Pull off the charred eggplant skin and slice off the stem and discard. If you baked the eggplant, scoop the flesh out with a spoon. Coarsely chop the eggplant flesh.

Combine the eggplant, garlic, lemon juice, and yogurt in the bowl of a food processor and purée until smooth. With the machine running, slowly pour in the olive oil. Add the parsley and pulse a few times. Season with salt and pepper to taste.

Make this dish at least an hour before serving so the flavors can develop. Taste and season again just before serving. Place the dip in a serving bowl and sprinkle the paprika over the top. The dip lasts for 5 days refrigerated, but will need to be reseasoned with salt after sitting in the refrigerator.

Resources

BEEKEEPING

The American Beekeeping Federation: www.abfnet.org

The Pollinator Partnership, for information on how to support pollinators and pollinating plants by discovering your "eco-region" and which plants to grow in your area: www.pollinator.org

Texas A&M University's honeybee information site: http://honeybee.tamu.edu

COMPOSTING

Worms Eat My Garbage: How to Set Up & Maintain a Worm Composting System, by Mary Appelhof (Kalamazoo, MI: Flower Press, 1997).

FAIR TRADE

Fair Trade, for information about fair trade certification and products: www.fairtrade.org

GARDENING

State extension schools, a nationwide educational network linked to the land-grant university in every state that has practical information and classes on gardening, health, nutrition, and agriculture: www.csrees.usda.gov/Extension/ to find your County Extension office.

For information on gardening, composting, and conservation, visit these websites for gardens with active conservation programs.

Berry Botanic Garden, Portland, OR: www.berrybot.org

Brooklyn Botanic Garden, Brooklyn, NY: www.bbg.org

Fairchild Tropical Botanic Garden, Coral Gables, FL: www.fairchildgarden.org

HEIRLOOMS

Native Seeds/SEARCH, for heirloom seeds and cultural preservation: www.nativeseeds.org

Rancho Gordo, for heirloom beans: www.ranchogordo.com

Seeds of Change, for heirloom seeds: www.seedsofchange.com

ASIAN INGREDIENTS

99 Ranch
Locations in CA, WA, and NV
www.99ranch.com

United Noodles
2015 E 24th Street
Minneapolis, MN 55404
www.unitednoodles.com

Uwajimaya Seattle
600 5th Avenue South
Seattle, WA 98104
www.uwajimaya.com

MIDDLE EASTERN INGREDIENTS

Ethnic Foods Co., to purchase Middle
Eastern and many other ethnic ingredients:
www.ethnicfoodsco.com

Kalamala, for Middle Eastern foods and
kitchenware: www.kalamala.com

Kalustyan's
123 Lexington Avenue
New York, NY 10016
www.kalustyans.com

Phoenicia Specialty Foods
12141 Westheimer Road
Houston, TX 77077
www.phoeniciafoods.com

LOCAL EATING

LocalHarvest, for information about
local and sustainably grown food resources
in your area, including farmers' markets and
CSAs, when you enter your zip code:
www.localharvest.org

Locavores, a San Francisco–based site
that provides information and resources for
eating locally wherever you are:
www.locavores.com

MAKING INFORMED
FOOD CHOICES

*Coming Home to Eat: The Pleasures and
Politics of Local Foods*, by Gary Paul Nabhan
(New York: Norton, 2002).

*Fast Food Nation: The Dark Side of the
All-American Meal*, by Eric Schlosser (New
York: Harper Perennial, 2002).

*The Omnivore's Dilemma: A Natural
History of Four Meals*, by Michael Pollan
(New York: Penguin, 2007).

What to Eat, by Marion Nestle (New
York: North Point Press, 2007).

PICKLING AND CANNING

Ball Blue Book of Preserving (Muncie, IN:
Alltrista Consumer Products, 2004).

Putting Food By, by Janet Greene (Lexington, MA: Stephen Greene Press, 1973).

SEAFOOD GUIDES

Environmental Defense Fund Seafood
Selector, for information on nature conservation and the best and worst seafoods to
buy: www.edf.org/page.cfm?tagID=1521

Monterey Bay Aquarium Seafood Watch,
for information on ocean conservation and
the best and worst seafoods to buy:
www.montereybayaquarium.org/cr/Seafood
Watch/web/sfw_factsheet.aspx

Natural Resources Defense Council,
for recipes using eco-friendly fish choices:
www.nrdc.org/water/oceans/gseafood.asp

SUSTAINABLE FOOD ISSUES

Center for Food Safety, a nonprofit food
policy watchdog that campaigns for sustainable food production:
www.centerforfoodsafety.org

Sustainable Table, an online magazine
about local and sustainable food, covering
a wide range of topics:
www.sustainabletable.org

WILD FORAGING

All That the Rain Promises, and More, by
David Arora (Berkeley, CA: Ten Speed Press,
1991).

*The Audubon Society Field Guide to North
American Mushrooms*, by Gary Lincoff (New
York: Knopf, 1981).

Mushrooms Demystified, by David Arora
(Berkeley, CA: Ten Speed Press, 1986).

Index